"Every day contemporary culture invites me to rush about
in a hundred different directions that tear at my soul.
I have found Eugene Peterson to have no patience for such crazed
busyness. Instead he shows me how to stay focused
on the long, biblical direction home to God."

CRAIG BARNES
author of *When God Interrupts*

"I thank God for *A Long Obedience*. It is a pioneer message,
first coming to us at a time when no one was talking
about either 'long' or 'obedience.' And while, thankfully,
others have added their voices in the intervening years,
A Long Obedience retains its prophetic edge for us who live
on the cusp of the twenty-first century. Rooted in the ancient
psalmist's Songs of Ascents, it invites us to journey with Jesus
into the rich spiritual landscape of 'righteousness and peace
and joy in the Holy Spirit.' "

RICHARD J. FOSTER
author of *Celebration of Discipline*
and *Streams of Living Water*

"There is a clean, bright rigor to honest life before God.
Burnishing the language of the Psalms, Eugene Peterson
makes that life sing like a taut wire. A long obedience
is the only path of discipleship to Jesus, and this is a message
we desperately need to hear and implement today."

DALLAS WILLARD
author of *The Divine Conspiracy*

"I've never read a book by Eugene Peterson
that didn't stir and challenge me."

MAX LUCADO
author of *In the Grip of Grace*

"Eugene Peterson's special gift is to stand beside us and keep our feet on the ground as he lifts our hearts to God and our minds to godliness. *A Long Obedience in the Same Direction*, which does this stunningly well, is also the best pathway into the Psalter you are likely to find. If, like me for twenty years, you find it hard to get into the Psalms, that is another reason to read, mark, learn and inwardly digest this brilliant book."

J. I. PACKER
author of *Knowing God*

"It has been said in today's instant society that evangelism has never been easier: it's *discipleship* that has never been harder. Eugene Peterson not only instructs us in his considerable wisdom about authentic discipleship, he helps us see the passion and excitement of living lives fully devoted to Jesus. And with the current torrent of interest in spirituality, his guidance on what constitutes genuine spirituality is pure gold."

REBECCA MANLEY PIPPERT
author of *Out of the Saltshaker*

"Bind this book in the burlap of servanthood: a course in the weak times, a celebration in the strong! Twenty years ago I first read this *tolle lege* book. Now it is a well-read friend who looks down from my Peterson shelf and daily asks: Are you faithful long-term? Are you going always in the same direction?"

CALVIN MILLER
author of *The Singer Trilogy*

"Words are weapons for good or ill, and Eugene H. Peterson uses them to wield the sword of Scripture to pierce our minds and hearts. He is one of God's most gifted wordsmiths, and we are privileged to have his work among us.

"I have constantly used his writings and concepts in my ministry; putting them to use in drama, teaching and books, and they have hugely enhanced my own gifting. Not least, those words have had a sweet influence in my own 'obedience in the same direction'! I am honored to endorse this Christian classic."

JILL P. BRISCOE
author of *Running on Empty*

"Into a world that does its best to deceive us into believing that *everything* changes, God speaks his unchanging Word. Ours is a time and a world that needs to hear in fresh ways all that that Word might mean if we would only listen. Eugene has listened. In this book he tells us all that he has heard about those fixed facets of that unchanging Word."

MICHAEL CARD
recording artist

"A wonderful book, one of the very best guides to the Psalms. Peterson's combination of passion and insight match the psalmists'. And he is very nearly as good a writer!"

TIM STAFFORD
author of *Knowing the Face of God*

"All of the marks of a classic—profound, timeless, life-impacting."

LEITH ANDERSON
author of *Leadership That Works*

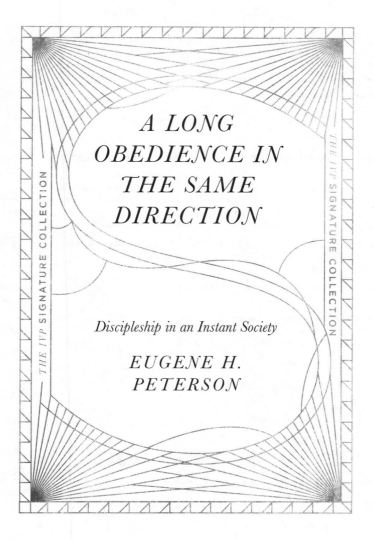

A LONG OBEDIENCE IN THE SAME DIRECTION

Discipleship in an Instant Society

*EUGENE H.
PETERSON*

An imprint of InterVarsity Press
Downers Grove, Illinois

InterVarsity Press
P.O. Box 1400, Downers Grove, IL 60515-1426
ivpress.com
email@ivpress.com

Commemorative Preface ©2019 by Leif Peterson
Second edition ©2000 by Eugene H. Peterson
First edition ©1980 by Inter-Varsity Christian Fellowship of the United States of America

Published in this format in 2021.

InterVarsity Press® is the book-publishing division of InterVarsity Christian Fellowship/USA®, a movement of students and faculty active on campus at hundreds of universities, colleges, and schools of nursing in the United States of America, and a member movement of the International Fellowship of Evangelical Students. For information about local and regional activities, visit intervarsity.org.

Scripture quotations, unless otherwise noted, are from THE MESSAGE, copyright © 1993, 1994, 1995, 1996, 2000, 2001, 2002 by Eugene H. Peterson. Used by permission of NavPress. All rights reserved. Represented by Tyndale House Publishers, Inc.

While any stories in this book are true, some names and identifying information may have been changed to protect the privacy of individuals.

Prayer #15 in Little Prayers and Finite Experience *by Paul Goodman. Volume twenty-four of The Religious Perspective Series edited by Ruth Nanda Anshen. Copyright ©1972 by The Estate of Paul Goodman. Reprinted by permission of Harper and Row Publishers, Inc.*

Cover design: David Fassett
Interior design: Cindy Kiple
Image: Mountain landscape photo © Kalen Emsley / unsplash.com

ISBN 978-0-8308-4863-8 (print)
ISBN 978-0-8308-5547-6 (digital)

Printed in the United States of America ∞

InterVarsity Press is committed to ecological stewardship and to the conservation of natural resources in all our operations. This book was printed using sustainably sourced paper.

Library of Congress Cataloging-in-Publication Data
Peterson, Eugene H., 1932-
A long obedience in the same direction: discipleship in an instant society/Eugene H. Peterson.—20th anniversary ed.
p. cm.
Includes bibliographical references.
ISBN 0-8308-2277-1 (cloth)—ISBN 0-8308-2257-7 (pbk.: alk. paper)
1. Bible. O.T. Psalms CXX-CXXXIV—Meditations. I. Title.
BS1430.4.P466 2000
223'.206—dc21

00-039580.

P	20	19	18	17	16	15	14	13	12	11	10	9	8	7	6
Y	38	37	36	35	34	33	32	31	30	29	28	27	26	25	24	23	22

For Lu and Peter
companions still in the long obedience

Contents

Commemorative Preface

A Eulogy for the Celebration of the
Resurrection of Eugene Peterson

LEIF PETERSON

Over the past few years, and especially more recently, thanks to the way social media has kept us increasingly connected, I've received a lot of messages from people wanting to express their appreciation for my dad. These messages, although personal and specific, are also similarly thematic.

This one, although an amalgam, is faithful to any number of notes I've received, some from people I remember or vaguely remember, some from people I never knew.

Dear Leif,

I heard recently that your dad is not doing well. I hope that's not true. There is probably no one on this planet that I think of more often than your dad. He intervened on my behalf when I was fourteen. At the time I had no idea what he'd done. Even now I really don't know any more than that he was the galvanizing force in changing the course of my life in a way that set me on a better path.

There are very few people who come to my mind as frequently as your father, not just the wisdom of his sermons, but his support of my mother that made my childhood slightly more stable, his intervention when life seemed untenable, and much more that I'm sure I have no knowledge of.

When you see him next please tell him that without his help I'm certain my life would not be the modest success that it is. And tell him thank you.

It was not uncommon in these notes to hear the words:
Your dad is the reason I became a minister.
Your dad saved my marriage.
Your dad saved my ministry.
Your dad saved my life.

The next time I would see my dad, usually on the Tuesdays I would always spend with him at the lake, I would read him these messages. After I was done reading, he would often rub his hands together and smile and nod pensively and say, "Oh, that's good. That's good."

In these times of mental decline, I don't know if he fully contextually understood who the sender was or the circumstances from the past that compelled them to write to him and convey that depth of appreciation. But I do know this: he knew that it was good. Not that he had done something good, but that when we are in relationship, with God and with others, good things inevitably happen. My dad's message was always that the good news always plays out best in relationships. Always in relationships.

The writer of Genesis tells us that at the end of each day of creation God looked around at the work that he'd done and saw that it was good. I think my dad did that a lot. He was always looking around, at the mountains, at the flowers, at the birds, and at the relationships forming and playing out all around him, and you could tell from the twinkle in his eyes what he was thinking. "Oh man, that's good. That's really good."

The writer of Genesis also tells us that on the seventh day of creation God rested from the work he'd completed. On October 22, surrounded by family, my dad reached the seventh day. And although we're going to miss him—a lot—that too is good.

When I was in high school I used to joke with my dad that he only had one sermon. And although it was a joke between us, I believed then, as I do now, that it is largely accurate. My dad had one message.

A few years ago there was a commissioning service in Colorado for the translation of the New Testament that my dad had completed. I was invited to say a few words. In preparation I couldn't shake that thought that for his whole life my dad only had one sermon—one message.

So I wrote a poem.

This is called "The Message."

The Message
It's almost laughable
how you fooled them.
How for thirty years, every week
you made them think
you were saying something new.
They thought you were
a magician. In your long black robe,
hiding so much up your ample sleeves,
always pulling something fresh
and making them think it was just
for them. And that's just
the beginning. There was more.
Casual conversations at church picnics,
unmemorable chats at the local Denny's
over eggs and toast. Counseling sessions
that saved marriages, maybe even lives.
And they didn't know what
a fraud you were. They didn't know
how simple it all was. They were blind
to your secret, only saw the magic
you performed, how you made the mysterious,
the ominous, the holy, into a cup of coffee,
how you made a cup of coffee into an act of grace,
how you could make
God into something that worked for them.

It's so funny that they didn't notice.
So many times I've wanted to
expose you. Tell them all what you've
been up to. And now you're doing it
again. You've got this new group fooled
into thinking you're worth millions.
They're printing it on T-shirts, coffee mugs,
message pads, a new version every week,
for some new flock. But, I must say this,
they've widened your audience. Now you're fooling
them all over the world, in churches, schools, homes,
and prisons. It's so funny.
Only my inheritance keeps me
from giving you away.
Because I alone know your secret.
I alone know what you've been doing.
How you've fooled them all, taking something
so simple, something a child could understand
and making it into a career, a vocation, an empire.
I know.
Because for fifty years you've
been telling me the secret. For fifty
years you've stealed into my room
at night and whispered softly to my
sleeping head. It's the same message
over and over and you don't vary
it one bit.
God loves you.
He's on your side.
He's coming after you.
He's relentless.

First Presbyterian Church, Kalispell, Montana
November 3, 2018

20th-Anniversary Preface

In the twenty years since I first wrote this book, enormous changes have taken place across the board all over the world and throughout the church. I find myself being told constantly and from almost every direction that I am in danger of becoming irrelevant if I don't stay current with the latest developments in computers and appliances and transportation and the media. And so as I sat down to revise *A Long Obedience in the Same Direction* for this twentieth-anniversary edition, I was prepared to do a lot of changing.

I have done hardly any. It turns out that there are some things that don't change. God doesn't change: he seeks and he saves. And our response to God as he reveals himself in Jesus doesn't change: we listen and we follow. Or we don't. When we are dealing with the basics—God and our need for God—we are at bedrock. We start each day at the beginning with no frills.

So the book comes out in this new edition substantially as I first wrote it. I added an epilogue to reaffirm the ways in which Scripture and prayer fuse to provide energy and direction to those of us who set out to follow Jesus. A few celebrity names have been replaced by new ones (celebrities change pretty rapidly!), and I have changed a few references to current affairs. But that's about it. It is reassuring to realize once again that we don't have to anxiously study the world around us in order to keep up with God and his ways with us.

The most conspicuous change has been the use of a fresh translation of the Holy Scriptures, *The Message,* that I have been

working on continuously since the publication of *A Long Obedience*. In fact, the fifteen Songs of Ascents (Psalms 120—134)
that provide the text here for developing "discipleship in an instant society" provided the impetus for embarking on the new
translation. All I had in mind at first was translating the Psalms
into the idiomatic North American language that I heard people
using on the streets and in the shopping malls and at football
games. I knew that following Jesus could never develop into a
"long obedience" without a deepening life of prayer and that
the Psalms had always been the primary means by which Christians learned to pray everything they lived, and live everything
they prayed over the long haul.

But the people I was around didn't pray the Psalms. That
puzzled me; Christians have *always* prayed the Psalms; why
didn't my friends and neighbors? Then I realized that it was because the language, cadenced and beautiful and harmonious,
seemed remote from their jerky and messy and discordant everyday lives. But when these Psalms were first prayed and written
by our Hebrew ancestors, they were every bit as jerky and messy
and discordant as anything we experience today. I wanted to
translate them from their Hebrew original and convey the raw,
rough and robust energy that is so characteristic of these
prayers. I wanted people to start *praying* them again, not just
admiring them from a distance, and thereby learn to pray everything they experienced and felt and thought as they followed
Jesus, not just what they thought was proper to pray in church.

And so it happened that the unintended consequence of the
writing of *A Long Obedience in the Same Direction* was this new
translation of the Songs of Ascents, and then all the Psalms and
the New Testament (and eventually the whole Bible). The inclu-
sion of that translation in this new edition completes the book in
a way I could not have anticipated twenty years ago.

1

DISCIPLESHIP

"What Makes You Think You Can Race Against Horses?"

*If you're worn out in this footrace with men, what
makes you think you can race against horses?*

JEREMIAH 12:5

---

*The essential thing "in heaven and earth" is . . .
that there should be long obedience in the same
direction; there thereby results, and has always
resulted in the long run, something which
has made life worth living.*

FRIEDRICH NIETZSCHE,
BEYOND GOOD AND EVIL

T his world is no friend to grace. A person who makes a commitment to Jesus Christ as Lord and Savior does not find a crowd immediately forming to applaud the decision or old friends spontaneously gathering around to offer congratulations and counsel. Ordinarily there is nothing directly hostile, but an accumulation of puzzled disapproval and agnostic indifference constitutes, nevertheless, surprisingly formidable opposition.

An old tradition sorts the difficulties we face in the life of faith into the categories of world, flesh and devil.[1] We are, for the most part, well warned of the perils of the flesh and the wiles of the devil. Their temptations have a definable shape and maintain a historical continuity. That doesn't make them any easier to resist; it does make them easier to recognize.

The world, though, is protean: each generation has the world to deal with in a new form. *World* is an atmosphere, a mood.[2] It is nearly as hard for a sinner to recognize the world's temptations as it is for a fish to discover impurities in the water. There is a sense, a feeling, that things aren't right, that the environment is not whole, but just what it is eludes analysis. We know that the spiritual atmosphere in which we live erodes faith, dissipates hope and corrupts love, but it is hard to put our finger on what is wrong.

Tourists and Pilgrims

One aspect of *world* that I have been able to identify as harmful to Christians is the assumption that anything worthwhile can be acquired at once. We assume that if something can be done at all, it can be done quickly and efficiently. Our attention spans have been conditioned by thirty-second commercials. Our sense of reality has been flattened by thirty-page abridgments.

It is not difficult in such a world to get a person interested in the message of the gospel; it is terrifically difficult to sustain the interest. Millions of people in our culture make decisions for Christ, but there is a dreadful attrition rate. Many claim to have been born again, but the evidence for mature Christian discipleship is slim. In our kind of culture anything, even news about God, can be sold if it is packaged freshly; but when it loses its novelty, it goes on the garbage heap. There is a great market for religious experience in our world; there is little enthusiasm for the patient acquisition of virtue, little inclination to sign up for a long apprenticeship in what earlier generations of Christians called holiness.

Religion in our time has been captured by the tourist mindset. Religion is understood as a visit to an attractive site to be made when we have adequate leisure. For some it is a weekly jaunt to church; for others, occasional visits to special services. Some, with a bent for religious entertainment and sacred diversion, plan their lives around special events like retreats, rallies and conferences. We go to see a new personality, to hear a new truth, to get a new experience and so somehow expand our otherwise humdrum lives. The religious life is defined as the latest and the newest: Zen, faith healing, human potential, parapsychology, successful living, choreography in the chancel, Armageddon. We'll try anything—until something else comes along.

I don't know what it has been like for pastors in other cultures and previous centuries, but I am quite sure that for a pastor in Western culture at the dawn of the twenty-first century, the aspect of *world* that makes the work of leading Christians in the way of faith most difficult is what Gore Vidal has analyzed as "today's passion for the immediate and the casual."[3] Everyone is in a hurry. The persons whom I lead in worship, among whom I counsel, visit, pray, preach and teach, want shortcuts. They want me to help them fill out the form that will get them instant credit (in eternity). They are impatient for results. They have adopted the lifestyle of a tourist and only want the high points. But a pastor is not a tour guide. I have no interest in telling apocryphal religious stories at and around dubiously identified sacred sites. The Christian life cannot mature under such conditions and in such ways.

Friedrich Nietzsche, who saw this area of spiritual truth at least with great clarity, wrote, "The essential thing 'in heaven and earth' is . . . that there should be long obedience in the same direction; there thereby results, and has always resulted in the long run, something which has made life worth living."[4] It is this "long obedience in the same direction" which the mood of the world does so much to discourage.

For recognizing and resisting the stream of the world's ways there are two biblical designations for people of faith that are extremely useful: *disciple* and *pilgrim*. *Disciple (mathētēs)* says we are people who spend our lives apprenticed to our master, Jesus Christ. We are in a growing-learning relationship, always. A disciple is a learner, but not in the academic setting of a schoolroom, rather at the work site of a craftsman. We do not acquire information about God but skills in faith.

Pilgrim (parepidēmos) tells us we are people who spend our lives going someplace, going to God, and whose path for getting there is the way, Jesus Christ. We realize that "this world is not my home" and set out for "the Father's house." Abraham, who "went out," is our archetype. Jesus, answering Thomas's question "Master, we have no idea where you're going. How do you expect us to know the road?" gives us directions: "I am the Road, also the Truth, also the Life. No one gets to the Father apart from me" (Jn 14:5-6). The letter to the Hebrews defines our program: "Do you see what this means—all these pioneers who blazed the way, all these veterans cheering us on? It means we'd better get on with it. Strip down, start running—and never quit! No extra spiritual fat, no parasitic sins. Keep your eyes on *Jesus,* who both began and finished this race we're in" (Heb 12:1-2).

A Dog-Eared Songbook

In the pastoral work of training people in discipleship and accompanying them in pilgrimage, I have found, tucked away in the Hebrew Psalter, an old dog-eared songbook. I have used it to provide continuity in guiding others in the Christian way and directing people of faith in the conscious and continuous effort that develops into maturity in Christ. The old songbook is called, in Hebrew, *shiray hammaloth*—Songs of Ascents. The songs are the psalms numbered 120 through 134 in the book of Psalms. These fifteen psalms were likely sung, possibly in sequence, by Hebrew pilgrims as they went up to Jerusalem to the great worship festivals. Topographically Jerusalem was the highest city in Palestine, and so all who traveled there spent much of their time ascending.[5] But the ascent was not only literal, it was also a metaphor: the trip to Jerusalem acted out a life lived upward toward God, an existence that advanced from one level to another in developing maturity—what Paul described as "the goal, where God is beckoning us onward—to Jesus" (Phil 3:14).

Three times a year faithful Hebrews made that trip (Ex 23:14-17; 34:22-24). The Hebrews were a people whose salvation had been accomplished in the exodus, whose identity had been defined at Sinai and whose preservation had been assured in the forty years of wilderness wandering. As such a people, they regularly climbed the road to Jerusalem to worship. They refreshed their memories of God's saving ways at the Feast of Passover in the spring; they renewed their commitments as God's covenanted people at the Feast of Pentecost in early summer; they responded as a blessed community to the best that God had for them at the Feast of Tabernacles in the autumn. They were a redeemed people, a commanded people, a blessed people. These foundational realities were preached and taught and praised at the annual feasts. Between feasts the people lived these realities in daily discipleship until the time came to go up to the mountain city again as pilgrims to renew the covenant.

This picture of the Hebrews singing these fifteen psalms as they left their routines of discipleship and made their way from towns and villages, farms and cities, as pilgrims up to Jerusalem has become embedded in the Christian devotional imagination. It is our best background for understanding life as a faith-journey.

We know that our Lord from a very early age traveled to Jerusalem for the annual feasts (Lk 2:41-42). We continue to identify with the first disciples, who "set out for Jerusalem. Jesus had a head start on them, and they were following, puzzled and not just a little afraid" (Mk 10:32). We also are puzzled and a little afraid, for there is wonder upon unexpected wonder on this road, and there are fearful specters to be met. Singing the fifteen psalms is a way both to express the amazing grace and to quiet the anxious fears.

There are no better "songs for the road" for those who travel the way of faith in Christ, a way that has so many continuities with the way of Israel. Since many (not all) essential items in Christian discipleship are incorporated in these songs, they provide a way to remember who we are and where we are going. I have not sought to produce scholarly expositions of these psalms but to offer practical meditations that use these tunes for stimulus, encouragement and guidance. If we learn to sing them well, they can be a kind of *vade mecum* for a Christian's daily walk.

Between the Times

Paul Tournier, in *A Place for You,* describes the experience of being in between—between the time we leave home and arrive at our destination; between the time we leave adolescence and arrive at adulthood; between the time we leave doubt and arrive at faith.[6] It is like the time when a trapeze artist lets go the bar and hangs in midair, ready to catch another support: it is a time of danger, of expectation, of uncertainty, of excitement, of extraordinary aliveness.

Christians will recognize how appropriately these psalms may be sung between the times: between the time we leave the world's environment and arrive at the Spirit's assembly; between the time we leave sin and arrive at holiness; between the time we leave home on Sunday morning and arrive in church with the company of God's people; between the time we leave the works of the law and arrive at justification by faith. They are songs of transition, brief hymns that provide courage, support and inner direction for getting us to where God is leading us in Jesus Christ.

Meanwhile the world whispers, "Why bother? There is plenty to enjoy without involving yourself in all that. The past is a graveyard—ignore it; the future is a holocaust—avoid it. There is no payoff for discipleship, there is no destination for pilgrimage. Get God the quick way; buy instant charisma." But other voices speak—if not more attractively, at least more truly. Thomas Szasz, in his therapy and writing, has attempted to revive respect for what he calls the "simplest and most ancient of human truths: namely, that life is an arduous and tragic struggle; that what we call 'sanity,' what we mean by 'not being schizophrenic,' has a great deal to do with competence, earned by struggling for excellence; with compassion, hard won by confronting conflict; and with modesty and patience, acquired through silence and suffering."[7] His testimony validates the decision of those who commit themselves to explore the world of the Songs of Ascents, who mine them for wisdom and sing them for cheerfulness.

These psalms were no doubt used in such ways by the multitudes Isaiah described as saying, "Come, let's climb God's mountain, go to the House of the God of Jacob. He'll show us the way he works so we can live the way we're made" (Is 2:3). They are also evidence of what Isaiah promised when he said, "You will sing! sing through an all-night holy feast; your hearts will burst with song, make music like the sounds of flutes on parade, en route to the mountain of God, on their way to the Rock of Israel" (Is 30:29).

Everyone who travels the road of faith requires assistance from time to time. We need cheering up when spirits flag; we need direction when the way is unclear. One of Paul Goodman's "little prayers" expresses our needs:

On the highroad to death
trudging, not eager to get
   to that city, yet the way is
   still too long for my patience

—teach me a travel song,
Master, to march along
   as we boys used to shout
   when I was a young scout.[8]

For those who choose to live no longer as tourists but as pilgrims, the Songs of Ascents combine all the cheerfulness of a travel song with the practicality of a guidebook and map. Their unpretentious brevity is excellently described by William Faulkner. "They are not monuments, but footprints. A monument only says, 'At least I got this far,' while a footprint says, 'This is where I was when I moved again.' "[9]

2

REPENTANCE

"I'm Doomed to Live in Meshech"

I'm in trouble. I cry to GOD,
desperate for an answer:
"Deliver me from the liars, GOD!
They smile so sweetly but lie through their teeth."
Do you know what's next, can you see what's coming,
all you barefaced liars?
Pointed arrows and burning coals
will be your reward.
I'm doomed to live in Meshech,
cursed with a home in Kedar.
My whole life lived camping
among quarreling neighbors.
I'm all for peace, but the minute
I tell them so, they go to war!

PSALM 120

Before a man can do things there must be things he will not do.

MENCIUS

P eople submerged in a culture swarming with lies and malice feel as if they are drowning in it: they can trust nothing they hear, depend on no one they meet. Such dissatisfaction with the world as it is is preparation for traveling in the way of Christian discipleship. The dissatisfaction, coupled with a longing for peace and truth, can set us on a pilgrim path of wholeness in God.

A person has to be thoroughly disgusted with the way things are to find the motivation to set out on the Christian way. As long as we think the next election might eliminate crime and establish justice or another scientific breakthrough might save the environment or another pay raise might push us over the edge of anxiety into a life of tranquillity, we are not likely to risk the arduous uncertainties of the life of faith. A person has to get fed up with the ways of the world before he, before she, acquires an appetite for the world of grace.

Psalm 120 is the song of such a person, sick with the lies and crippled with the hate, a person doubled up in pain over what is going on in the world. But it is not a mere outcry, it is pain that penetrates through despair and stimulates a new beginning—a journey to God that becomes a life of peace.

The fifteen Songs of Ascents describe elements common to all those who apprentice themselves to the Lord Christ and who travel in the Christian way. This first of them is the prod that gets them going. It is not a beautiful song—there is nothing either hauntingly melancholy or lyrically happy in it. It is harsh. It is discordant. But it gets things started.

Lies Without Error

I'm in trouble is the opening phrase. The last word is *war.* Not a happy song but an honest and necessary one.

Men are set against each other. Women are at each other's throats. We are taught rivalry from the womb. The world is restless, always spoiling for a fight. No one seems to know how to live in healthy relationships. We persist in turning every community into a sect, every enterprise into a war. We realize, in fugitive moments, that we were made for something different and better—"I'm all for peace"—but there is no confirmation of that realization in our environment, no encouragement of it in our experience. "I'm all for peace; but the minute I tell them so, they go to war!"

The distress that begins and ends the song is the painful awakening to the no-longer-avoidable reality that we have been lied to. The world, in fact, is not as it had been represented to us. Things are not all right as they are, and they are not getting any better.

We have been told the lie ever since we can remember: human beings are basically nice and good. Everyone is born equal and innocent and self-sufficient. The world is a pleasant, harmless place. We are born free. If we are in chains now, it is someone's fault, and we can correct it with just a little more intelligence or effort or time.

How we can keep on believing this after so many centuries of evidence to the contrary is difficult to comprehend, but nothing we do and nothing anyone else does to us seems to disenchant us from the spell of the lie. We keep expecting things to get better somehow. And when they don't, we whine like spoiled children who don't get their way. We accumulate resentment that

stores up in anger and erupts in violence. Convinced by the lie
that what we are experiencing is unnatural, an exception, we de-
vise ways to escape the influence of what other people do to us
by getting away on a vacation as often as we can. When the vacation is over, we get back into the flow of things again, our na-
iveté renewed that everything is going to work out all right—
only to once more be surprised, hurt, bewildered when it
doesn't. The lie ("everything is OK") covers up and perpetuates
the deep wrong, disguises the violence, the war, the rapacity.

Christian consciousness begins in the painful realization that
what we had assumed was the truth is in fact a lie. Prayer is immediate: "Deliver me from the liars, God! They smile so sweetly
but lie through their teeth." Rescue me from the lies of advertisers who claim to know what I need and what I desire, from the
lies of entertainers who promise a cheap way to joy, from the lies
of politicians who pretend to instruct me in power and morality,
from the lies of psychologists who offer to shape my behavior
and my morals so that I will live long, happily and successfully,
from the lies of religionists who "heal the wounds of this people
lightly," from the lies of moralists who pretend to promote me
to the office of captain of my fate, from the lies of pastors who
"get rid of God's command so you won't be inconvenienced in
following the religious fashions!" (Mk 7:8). Rescue me from the
person who tells me of life and omits Christ, who is wise in the
ways of the world and ignores the movement of the Spirit.

The lies are impeccably factual. They contain no errors. There
are no distortions or falsified data. But they are lies all the same,
because they claim to tell us who we are and omit everything
about our origin in God and our destiny in God. They talk
about the world without telling us that God made it. They tell
us about our bodies without telling us that they are temples of
the Holy Spirit. They instruct us in love without telling us about

the God who loves us and gave himself for us.

Lightning Illuminating the Crossroads

The single word *God* occurs only twice in this psalm, but it is the clue to the whole. God, once admitted to the consciousness, fills the entire horizon. God, revealed in his creative and redemptive work, exposes all the lies. The moment the word *God* is uttered, the world's towering falsehood is exposed—we see the truth. The truth about me is that God made and loves me. The truth about those sitting beside me is that God made them and loves them, and each one is therefore my neighbor. The truth about the world is that God rules and provides for it. The truth about what is wrong with the world is that I and the neighbor sitting beside me have sinned in refusing to let God be for us, over us and in us. The truth about what is at the center of our lives and of our history is that Jesus Christ was crucified on the cross for our sins and raised from the tomb for our salvation and that we can participate in new life as we believe in him, accept his mercy, respond to his love, attend to his commands.

John Baillie wrote, "I am sure that the bit of the road that most requires to be illuminated is the point where it forks."[1] The psalmist's *God* is a lightning flash illuminating just such a crossroads. Psalm 120 is the decision to take one way over against the other. It is the turning point marking the transition from a dreamy nostalgia for a better life to a rugged pilgrimage of discipleship in faith, from complaining about how bad things are to pursuing all things good.

This decision is said and sung on every continent in every language. The decision has been realized in every sort of life in every century in the long history of humankind. The decision is quietly (and sometimes not so quietly) announced from thousands of Christian pulpits all over the world each Sunday morning. The decision is witnessed by millions in homes, factories, schools, businesses, offices and fields every day of every week. The people who make the decision and take delight in it are the people called Christians.

A No That Is a Yes

The first step toward God is a step away from the lies of the world. It is a renunciation of the lies we have been told about ourselves and our neighbors and our universe. "I'm doomed to live in Meshech, cursed with a home in Kedar! My whole life lived camping among quarreling neighbors." Meshech and Kedar are place names: Meshech a far-off tribe, thousands of miles from Palestine in southern Russia; Kedar a wandering Bedouin tribe of barbaric reputation along Israel's borders. They represent the strange and the hostile. Paraphrased, the cry is, "I live in the midst of hoodlums and wild savages; this world is not my home and I want out."

The usual biblical word describing the no we say to the world's lies and the yes we say to God's truth is *repentance*. It is always and everywhere the first word in the Christian life. John the Baptist's preaching was "Repent, for the kingdom of heaven is at hand" (Mt 3:2 RSV). Jesus' first preaching was the same: "Repent, for the kingdom of heaven is at hand" (Mt 4:17 RSV). Peter concluded his first sermon with "Repent, and be baptized" (Acts 2:38 RSV). In the last book of the Bible the message to the seventh church is "be zealous and repent" (Rev 3:19 RSV).

Repentance is not an emotion. It is not feeling sorry for your sins. It is a decision. It is deciding that you have been wrong in supposing that you could manage your own life and be your own god; it is deciding that you were wrong in thinking that you had, or could get, the strength, education and training to make it on your own; it is deciding that you have been told a pack of lies about yourself and your neighbors and your world. And it is deciding that God in Jesus Christ is telling you the truth. Repentance is a realization that what God wants from you and what you want from God are not going to be achieved by doing the same old things, thinking the same old thoughts. Repentance is a decision to follow Jesus Christ and become his pilgrim in the path of peace.

Repentance is the most practical of all words and the most practical of all acts. It is a feet-on-the-ground kind of word. It puts a person in touch with the reality that God creates. Elie Wiesel, referring to the stories of the Hasidim, says that in the tales by Israel of Rizhim one motif recurs again and again: A traveler loses his way in the forest; it is dark and he is afraid. Danger lurks behind every tree. A storm shatters the silence. The fool looks at the lightning, the wise man at the road that lies—illuminated—before him.[2]

Whenever we say no to one way of life that we have long been used to, there is pain. But when the way of life is in fact a way of death, a way of war, the quicker we leave it the better. There is a condition that sometimes develops in our bodies called adhesions—parts of our internal organs become attached to other parts. The condition has to be corrected by a surgical procedure—a decisive intervention. The procedure hurts, but the results are healthy. As the Jerusalem Bible puts verses 3-4, "How will he [God] pay back the false oath?/of a faithless tongue/ With war arrows hardened/ over red-hot charcoal!" Emily Dickinson's spare sentence is an epigraph: "Renunciation—the piercing virtue!"

God's arrows are judgments aimed at provoking repentance. The pain of judgment called down against evildoers could turn them also from their deceitful and violent ways to join our pilgrim on the way of peace. Any hurt is worth it that puts us on the path of peace, setting us free for the pursuit, in Christ, of eternal life. It is the action that follows the realization that history is not a blind alley, guilt not an abyss. It is the discovery that there is always a way that leads out of distress—a way that begins in repentance, or turning to God. Whenever we find God's people living in distress, there is always someone who provides this hope-charged word, showing the reality of a different day: "On that day there will be a highway all the way from Egypt to Assyria: Assyrians will have free range in Egypt, and Egyptians in Assyria. No longer rivals, they'll worship together, Egyptians and Assyrians" (Is 19:23). All Israel knew of Assyria was war—the vision shows them at worship. Repentance is the catalytic agent for the change. Dismay is transformed into what a later prophet would describe as gospel.

The whole history of Israel is set in motion by two such acts of world-rejection, which freed the people for an affirmation of God: "the rejection of Mesopotamia in the days of Abraham and the rejection of Egypt in the days of Moses."[3] All the wisdom and strength of the ancient world were in Mesopotamia and Egypt. But Israel said no to them. Despite the prestige, the vaunted and uncontested greatness, there was something foundationally alien and false in those cultures: "I'm all for peace; but the minute I tell them so, they go to war!" Mesopotamian power and Egyptian wisdom were strength and intelligence divorced from God, put to the wrong ends and producing all the wrong results.

Modern interpretations of history are variations on the lies of the Mesopotamians and Egyptians in which, as Abraham Heschel describes it, "man reigns supreme, with the forces of nature as his only possible adversaries. Man is alone, free, and growing stronger. God is either nonexistent or unconcerned. It is human initiative that makes history, and it is primarily by force that constellations change. Man can attain his own salvation."[4]

So Israel said no and became a pilgrim people, picking a path of peace and righteousness through the battlefields of falsehood and violence, finding a path to God through the labyrinth of sin.

We know that Israel, in saying that no, did not miraculously return to Eden and live in primitive innocence, or mystically inhabit a heavenly city and live in supernatural ecstasy. They worked and played, suffered and sinned in the world as everyone else did, and as Christians still do. But they were now *going* someplace—they were going to God. The truth of God explained their lives, the grace of God fulfilled their lives, the forgiveness of God renewed their lives, the love of God blessed their lives. The no released them to a freedom that was diverse and glorious. The judgment of God invoked against the people of Meshech and Kedar was, in fact, a sharply worded invitation to repentance, asking them to join in the journey.

Among the more fascinating pages of American history are those that tell the stories of the immigrants to these shores in the nineteenth century. Thousands upon thousands of people, whose lives in Europe had become mean and poor, persecuted and wretched, left. They had heard of a place where a new start could be made. They had gotten reports of a land where the environment was a challenge instead of an oppression. The stories continue to be told in many families, keeping alive the memory of the event that made an American out of what was a German or an Italian or a Scot.

My grandfather left Norway a hundred years ago in the midst of a famine. His wife and ten children remained behind until he could return and get them. He came to Pittsburgh and worked in the steel mills for two years until he had enough money to go back and get his family. When he returned with them he didn't stay in Pittsburgh, although it had served his purposes well enough the first time; he traveled on to Montana, plunging into new land, looking for a better place.

In all these immigrant stories there are mixed parts of escape and adventure: the escape from an unpleasant situation, the adventure of a far better way of life, free for new things, open for growth and creativity. Every Christian has some variation on this immigrant plot to tell.

"I'm doomed to live in Meshech, cursed with a home in Kedar! My whole life lived camping among quarreling neighbors." But we don't have to live there any longer. Repentance, the first word in Christian immigration, sets us on the way to traveling in the light. It is a rejection that is also an acceptance, a leaving that develops into an arriving, a no to the world that is a yes to God.

3

PROVIDENCE

"GOD Guards You from Every Evil"

I look up to the mountains;
does my strength come from mountains?
No, my strength comes from GOD,
who made heaven, and earth, and mountains.
He won't let you stumble,
your Guardian God won't fall asleep.
Not on your life!
Israel's Guardian will never doze or sleep.
GOD's your Guardian,
right at your side to protect you—
Shielding you from sunstroke,
sheltering you from moonstroke.
GOD guards you from every evil,
he guards your very life.
He guards you when you leave and when you return,
he guards you now, he guards you always.

PSALM 121

But to deviate from the truth for the sake of some prospect of hope
of our own can never be wise, however slight that deviation may be.
It is not our judgement of the situation
which can show us what is wise,
but only the truth of the Word of God.
Here alone lies the promise of God's faithfulness and help.
It will always be true that the wisest course for the disciple
is always to abide solely by the Word of God in all simplicity.

DIETRICH BONHOEFFER

The moment we say no to the world and yes to God, all our problems are solved, all our questions answered, all our troubles over. Nothing can disturb the tranquillity of the soul at peace with God. Nothing can interfere with the blessed assurance that all is well between me and my Savior. Nothing and no one can upset the enjoyable relationship that has been established by faith in Jesus Christ. We Christians are among that privileged company of persons who don't have accidents, who don't have arguments with our spouses, who aren't misunderstood by our peers, whose children do not disobey us.

If any of those things should happen—a crushing doubt, a squall of anger, a desperate loneliness, an accident that puts us in the hospital, an argument that puts us in the doghouse, a rebellion that puts us on the defensive, a misunderstanding that puts us in the wrong—it is a sign that something is wrong with our relationship with God. We have, consciously or unconsciously, retracted our yes to God; and God, impatient with our fickle faith, has gone off to take care of someone more deserving of his attention.

Is that what you believe? If it is, I have some incredibly good news for you. You are wrong.

To be told we are wrong is sometimes an embarrassment, even a humiliation. We want to run and hide our heads in shame. But there are times when finding out we are wrong is sudden and immediate relief, and we can lift up our heads in hope. No longer do we have to keep doggedly trying to do something that isn't working.

A few years ago I was in my backyard with my lawnmower tipped on its side. I was trying to get the blade off so I could sharpen it. I had my biggest wrench attached to the nut but couldn't budge it. I got a four-foot length of pipe and slipped it over the wrench handle to give me leverage, and I leaned on that—still unsuccessfully. Next I took a large rock and banged on the pipe. By this time I was beginning to get emotionally involved with my lawnmower.

Then my neighbor walked over and said that he had a lawnmower like mine once and that, if he remembered correctly, the threads on the bolt went the other way. I reversed my exertions and, sure enough, the nut turned easily.

I was glad to find out I was wrong. I was saved from frustration and failure. I would never have gotten the job done, no matter how hard I tried, doing it my way.

Psalm 121 is a quiet voice gently and kindly telling us that we are, perhaps, wrong in the way we are going about the Christian life, and then, very simply, showing us the right way. As such it is the necessary sequel to the previous psalm, which gets us started on the Christian way. It put a name to the confused and bewildering feelings of alienation and distrust that made us dissatisfied and restless in a way of life that ignores or rejects God, and prodded us into the repentance that renounces the "devil and all his works" and affirms the way of faith in Jesus Christ.

But no sooner have we plunged, expectantly and enthusiastically, into the river of Christian faith than we get our noses full of water and come up coughing and choking. No sooner do we confidently stride out onto the road of faith than we trip on an obstruction and fall to the hard surface, bruising our knees and elbows. For many, the first great surprise of the Christian life is in the form of troubles we meet. Somehow it is not what we had supposed: we had expected something quite different; we had our minds set on Eden or on New Jerusalem. We are rudely awakened to something very different, and we look around for help, scanning the horizon for someone who will give us aid: "I look up to the mountains; does my strength come from mountains?"

Psalm 121 is the neighbor coming over and telling us that we are doing it the wrong way, looking in the wrong place for help. Psalm 121 is addressed to those of us who, "disregarding God, gaze to a distance all around them, and make long and devious circuits in quest of remedies to their troubles."[1]

Travelers' Advisory

Three possibilities for harm to travelers are referred to in the psalm. A person traveling on foot can at any moment step on a loose stone and sprain his ankle. A person traveling on foot under protracted exposure to a hot sun, can become faint with sunstroke. And a person traveling for a long distance on foot, under the pressures of fatigue and anxiety, can become emotionally ill, which was described by ancient writers as moonstroke (or by us as *lunacy*). We can update the list of dangers. Provisions for law and order can break down with dismaying ease: a crazed person with a handgun or piece of explosive can turn the computerized travel plans of three hundred air passengers into instant anarchy. Disease can break through our pharmaceutical defenses and invade our bodies with crippling pain and death. An accident—in an automobile, from a stepladder, on an athletic field—can without warning interrupt our carefully laid plans. We take precautions by learning safety rules, fastening our seatbelts and taking out insurance policies. But we cannot guarantee security.

In reference to these hazards the psalm says, "He won't let

you stumble, . . . GOD's your guardian . . . shielding you from
sunstroke, sheltering you from moonstroke." Are we to conclude then that Christians never sprain their ankles, never get
sunstroke, never have any emotional problems? That is what it
sounds like. Yet we know of plenty of instances to the contrary.
Some of the best Christians I know have sprained their ankles,
have fainted, have been overwrought with anxiety. Put that way,
either I'm wrong (these people I thought were Christians really
weren't and therefore the psalm doesn't apply to them) or the
psalm is wrong (God doesn't do what the psalm claims).

Help from the Hills?

But neither the psalm nor our experience is so easily disposed of.
A psalm that has enjoyed high regard among Christians so long
must have truth in it that is verified in Christian living. Let's
return to the psalm: The person set on the way of faith gets into
trouble, looks around for help ("I look up to the mountains")
and asks a question: "Does my strength come from moutains?"
As this person of faith looks around at the hills for help, what is
he, what is she, going to see?

Some magnificent scenery, for one thing. Is there anything
more inspiring than a ridge of mountains silhouetted against the
sky? Does any part of this earth promise more in terms of majesty and strength, of firmness and solidity, than the mountains?
But a Hebrew would see something else. During the time this
psalm was written and sung, Palestine was overrun with popular
pagan worship. Much of this religion was practiced on hilltops.
Shrines were set up, groves of trees were planted, sacred prosti-
tutes both male and female were provided; persons were lured
to the shrines to engage in acts of worship that would enhance
the fertility of the land, would make you feel good, would protect you from evil. There were nostrums, protections, spells and

enchantments against all the perils of the road. Do you fear the sun's heat? Go to the sun priest and pay for protection against the sun god. Are you fearful of the malign influence of moonlight? Go to the moon priestess and buy an amulet. Are you haunted by the demons that can use any pebble under your foot to trip you? Go to the shrine and learn the magic formula to ward off the mischief. Whence shall my help come? from Baal? from Asherah? from the sun priest? from the moon priestess?[2]

They must have been a shabby lot: immoral, diseased, drunken—frauds and cheats all. The legends of Baal are full of the tales of his orgies, the difficulty of rousing him out of a drunken sleep to get his attention. Elijah taunting the priests of Baal ("You don't suppose that he has overslept do you, and needs to be waked up?" 1 Kings 18:27) is the evidence. But shabby or not, they promised help. A traveler in trouble would hear their offer.

That is the kind of thing a Hebrew, set out on the way of faith twenty-five hundred years ago, would have seen on the hills. It is what disciples still see. A person of faith encounters trial or tribulation and cries out "Help!" We lift our eyes to the mountains, and offers of help, instant and numerous, appear. "Does my strength come from mountains?" No. "My strength comes from GOD, who made heaven, and earth, and mountains."

A look to the hills for help ends in disappointment. For all their majesty and beauty, for all their quiet strength and firmness, they are finally just hills. And for all their promises of safety against the perils of the road, for all the allurements of their priests and priestesses, they are all, finally, lies. As Jeremiah put it: "Truly the hills are a delusion, the orgies on the mountains" (Jer 3:23 RSV).[3]

And so Psalm 121 says no. It rejects a worship of nature, a religion of stars and flowers, a religion that makes the best of what it finds on the hills; instead it looks to the Lord who made heaven and earth. Help comes from the Creator, not from the creation. The Creator is always awake: he will never doze or sleep. Baal took long naps, and one of the jobs of the priests was to wake him up when someone needed his attention—and they were not always successful. The Creator is Lord over time: he "guards you when you leave and when you return," your beginnings and your endings. He is with you when you set out on your way; he is still with you when you arrive at your destination. You don't need to, in the meantime, get supplementary help from the sun or the moon. The Creator is Lord over all natural and supernatural forces: he made them. Sun, moon and rocks have no spiritual power. They are not able to inflict evil upon us: we need not fear any supernatural assault from any of them. "GOD guards you from every evil."

The promise of the psalm—and both Hebrews and Christians have always read it this way—is not that we shall never stub our toes but that no injury, no illness, no accident, no distress will have evil power over us, that is, will be able to separate us from God's purposes in us.

No literature is more realistic and honest in facing the harsh facts of life than the Bible. At no time is there the faintest suggestion that the life of faith exempts us from difficulties. What it promises is preservation from all the evil in them. On every page of the Bible there is recognition that faith encounters troubles. The sixth petition in the Lord's Prayer is "Lead us not into temptation, but deliver us from evil." That prayer is answered every day, sometimes many times a day, in the lives of those who walk in the way of faith. St. Paul wrote, "No test or temptation that comes your way is beyond the course of what others have had to face. All you need to remember is that God will never let you down; he'll never let you be pushed past your limit; he'll always be there to help you come through it" (1 Cor 10:13).

Three times in Psalm 121 God is referred to by the personal name Yahweh, translated as GOD. Eight times he is described as the *guardian,* or as the one who guards. He is not an impersonal executive giving orders from on high; he is present help every step of the way we travel. Do you think the way to tell the story of the Christian journey is to describe its trials and tribulations? It is not. It is to name and to describe God who preserves, accompanies and rules us.

All the water in all the oceans cannot sink a ship unless it gets inside. Nor can all the trouble in the world harm us unless it gets within us. That is the promise of the psalm: "GOD guards you from every evil." Not the demon in the loose stone, not the fierce attack of the sun god, not the malign influence of the moon goddess—not any of these can separate you from God's call and purpose. From the time of your repentance that got you out of Kedar and Meshech to the time of your glorification with the saints in heaven, you are safe: "GOD guards you from every evil." None of the things that happen to you, none of the troubles you encounter, have any power to get between you and God, dilute his grace in you, divert his will from you (see Rom 8:28, 31-32).

The only serious mistake we can make when illness comes, when anxiety threatens, when conflict disturbs our relationships with others is to conclude that God has gotten bored looking after us and has shifted his attention to a more exciting Christian, or that God has become disgusted with our meandering obedience and decided to let us fend for ourselves for a while, or that God has gotten too busy fulfilling prophecy in the Middle East to take time now to sort out the complicated mess we have gotten ourselves into. That is the *only* serious mistake we can make. It is the mistake that Psalm 121 prevents: the mistake of supposing that God's interest in us waxes and wanes in response to our spiritual temperature.

The great danger of Christian discipleship is that we should have two religions: a glorious, biblical Sunday gospel that sets us free from the world, that in the cross and resurrection of Christ makes eternity alive in us, a magnificent gospel of Genesis and Romans and Revelation; and, then, an everyday religion that we make do with during the week between the time of leaving the world and arriving in heaven. We save the Sunday gospel for the big crises of existence. For the mundane trivialities—the times when our foot slips on a loose stone, or the heat of the sun gets too much for us, or the influence of the moon gets us down—we use the everyday religion of the *Reader's Digest* reprint, advice from a friend, an Ann Landers column, the huckstered wisdom of a talk-show celebrity. We practice patent-medicine religion. We know that God created the universe and has accomplished our eternal salvation. But we can't believe that he condescends to watch the soap opera of our daily trials and tribulations; so we purchase our own remedies for that. To ask him to deal with what troubles us each day is like asking a famous surgeon to put iodine on a scratch.

But Psalm 121 says that the same faith that works in the big things works in the little things. The God of Genesis 1 who brought light out of darkness is also the God of this day who guards you from every evil.

Traveling Companion

The Christian life is not a quiet escape to a garden where we can walk and talk uninterruptedly with our Lord, not a fantasy trip to a heavenly city where we can compare our blue ribbons and gold medals with those of others who have made it to the winners' circle. To suppose that, or to expect that, is

to turn the nut the wrong way. The Christian life is going to
God. In going to God Christians travel the same ground that
everyone else walks on, breathe the same air, drink the same
water, shop in the same stores, read the same newspapers, are
citizens under the same governments, pay the same prices for
groceries and gasoline, fear the same dangers, are subject to
the same pressures, get the same distresses, are buried in the
same ground.

The difference is that each step we walk, each breath we
breathe, we know we are preserved by God, we know we are accompanied by God, we know we are ruled by God; and therefore no matter what doubts we endure or what accidents we
experience, the Lord will guard us from every evil, he guards
our very life. We know the truth of Luther's hymn:

> And though this world, with devils filled
> Should threaten to undo us,
> We will not fear, for God hath willed
> His truth to triumph through us.
> The prince of darkness grim,
> We tremble not for him;
> His rage we can endure,
> For lo! his doom is sure;
> One little word shall fell him.

We Christians believe that life is created and shaped by God and
that the life of faith is a daily exploration of the constant and
countless ways in which God's grace and love are experienced.

Psalm 121, learned early and sung repeatedly in the walk with
Christ, clearly defines the conditions under which we live out
our discipleship—which, in a word, is God. Once we get this
psalm in our hearts it will be impossible for us to gloomily suppose that being a Christian is an unending battle against omi-

nous forces that at any moment may break through and overpower us. Faith is not a precarious affair of chance escape from satanic assaults. It is the solid, massive, secure experience of God, who keeps all evil from getting inside us, who guards our life, who guards us when we leave and when we return, who guards us now, who guards us always.

4

WORSHIP

"Let's Go to the House of GOD"

When they said, "Let's go to the house of GOD,"
my heart leaped for joy.
And now we're here, oh Jerusalem,
inside Jerusalem's walls!
Jerusalem, well-built city,
built as a place for worship!
The city to which the tribes ascend,
all GOD's tribes go up to worship,
To give thanks to the name of GOD—
this is what it means to be Israel.
Thrones for righteous judgment
are set there, famous David-thrones.
Pray for Jerusalem's peace!
Prosperity to all you Jerusalem-lovers!
Friendly insiders, get along!
Hostile outsiders, keep your distance!
For the sake of my family and friends,
I say it again: live in peace!
For the sake of the house of our God, GOD,
I'll do my very best for you.

PSALM 122

There is something morally repulsive about
modern activistic theories which deny contemplation
and recognize nothing but struggle. For them not a single moment
has value in itself, but is only a means for what follows.

NICOLAS BERDYAEV

One of the afflictions of pastoral work has been to listen, with a straight face, to all the reasons people give for not going to church:

"My mother made me when I was little."

"There are too many hypocrites in the church."

"It's the only day I have to sleep in."

There was a time when I responded to such statements with simple arguments that exposed them as flimsy excuses. Then I noticed that it didn't make any difference. If I showed the inadequacy of one excuse, three more would pop up in its place. So I don't respond anymore. I listen (with a straight face) and go home and pray that person will one day find the one sufficient reason for going to church, which is God. I go about my work hoping that what I do and say will be usable by the Holy Spirit to create in that person a determination to worship God in a Christian community.

Many people do: they decide to worship God, faithfully and devoutly. It is one of the important acts in a life of discipleship. And what is far more interesting than the reasons (excuses) people give for not worshiping is discovering the reasons they do.

Psalm 122 is the song of a person who decides to go to church and worship God. It is a sample of the complex, diverse and worldwide phenomenon of worship that is common to all Christians. It is an excellent instance of what happens when a person worships.

Psalm 122 is third in the sequence of the Songs of Ascents.

Psalm 120 is the psalm of repentance—the one that gets us out of an environment of deceit and hostility and sets us on our way to God. Psalm 121 is the psalm of trust—a demonstration of how faith resists patent-medicine remedies to trials and tribulations and determinedly trusts God to work out his will and "guard you from every evil" in the midst of difficulty. Psalm 122 is the psalm of worship—a demonstration of what people of faith everywhere and always do: gather to an assigned place and worship their God.

An Instance of the Average

The first line catches many by surprise: "When they said, 'Let's go to the house of GOD,' my heart leaped for joy." But it shouldn't. Worship is the most popular thing that Christians do. A great deal of what we call Christian behavior has become part of our legal system and is embedded in our social expectations, both of which have strong coercive powers. If we removed all laws from society and eliminated all consequences for antisocial acts, we don't know how much murder, how much theft, how much perjury and falsification would take place. But we do know that much of what we commonly describe as Christian behavior is not volitional at all—it is enforced.

But worship is not forced. Everyone who worships does so because he or she wants to. There are, to be sure, a few temporary coercions—children and spouses who attend church because another has decided that they must. But these coercions are short-lived, a few years at most. Most Christian worship is voluntary.

An excellent way to test people's values is to observe what we do when we don't *have* to do anything, how we spend our leisure time, how we spend our extra money. Even in a time when church attendance is not considered to be on the upswing in the

United States, the numbers are impressive. There are more people at worship on any given Sunday, for instance, than are at all the football games or on the golf links or fishing or taking walks in the woods. Worship is the single most popular act in this land.

So when we hear the psalmist say, "When they said, 'Let's go to the house of GOD,' my heart leaped for joy," we are not listening to the phony enthusiasm of a propagandist drumming up business for worship; we are witnessing what is typical of most Christians in most places at most times. This is not an exception to which we aspire; it is an instance of the average.

A Framework

Why do we do it? Why is there so much voluntary and faithful worship by Christians? Why is it that we never find a Christian life without, in the background somewhere, an act of worship, never find Christian communities without also finding Christian worship? Why is it that worship is the common background to all Christian existence and that it is so faithfully and willingly practiced? The psalm singles out three items: worship gives us a workable structure for life; worship nurtures our need to be in relationship with God; worship centers our attention on the decisions of God.

Worship gives us a workable structure for life. The psalm says, "Jerusalem, well-built city, built as a place for worship! The city to which the tribes ascend, all GOD's tribes go up to worship." Jerusalem, for a Hebrew, was *the* place of worship (only incidentally was it the geographical center of the country and the political seat of authority). The great worship festivals to which everyone came at least three times a year were held in Jerusalem. In Jerusalem everything that God said was remembered and celebrated. When you went to Jerusalem, you encountered the great foundational realities: God created you, God redeemed you, God provided for you. In Jerusalem you saw in ritual and heard proclaimed in preaching the powerful history-shaping truth that God forgives our sins and makes it possible to live without guilt and with purpose. In Jerusalem all the scattered fragments of experience, all the bits and pieces of truth and feeling and perception were put together in a single whole.

The King James Version translates this sentence "Jerusalem is builded as a city that is compact together." Earlier Coverdale had translated the latter phrase as "that is at unity with itself." The city itself was a kind of architectural metaphor for what worship is: All the pieces of masonry fit compactly, all the building stones fit harmoniously. There were no loose stones, no leftover pieces, no awkward gaps in the walls or towers. It was well built, compactly built, skillfully built, "at unity with itself."

What is true architecturally is also true socially, for the sentence continues, "to which the tribes ascend, all GOD's tribes." In worship all the different tribes functioned as a single people in harmonious relationship. In worship, though we have come from different places and out of various conditions, we are demonstrably after the same things, saying the same things, doing the same things. With all our differing levels of intelligence and wealth, background and language, rivalries and resentments, still in worship we are gathered into a single whole. Outer quarrels and misunderstandings and differences pale into insignificance as the inner unity of what God builds in the act of worship is demonstrated.

When a person is confused and things refuse to fit together, she sometimes announces a need to get out of noise and turbulence, to get away from all the hassle and "get my head together." When she succeeds in doing this, we call that person "put together." All the parts are there, nothing is left out, nothing is out of proportion, everything fits into a workable frame.

As I entered a home to make a pastoral visit, the person I came to see was sitting at a window embroidering a piece of cloth held taut on an oval hoop. She said, "Pastor, while waiting for you to come I realized what's wrong with me—I don't have a frame. My feelings, my thoughts, my activities—everything is loose and sloppy. There is no border to my life. I never know where I am. I need a frame for my life like this one I have for my embroidery."

How do we get that framework, that sense of solid structure so that we know where we stand and are therefore able to do our work easily and without anxiety? Christians go to worship. Week by week we enter the place compactly built, "to which the tribes ascend," and get a working definition for life: the way God created us, the ways he leads us. We know where we stand.

A Command

Another reason Christians keep returning to worship is that it nurtures our need to be in relationship with God. Worship is the place where we obey the command to praise God: "To give thanks to the name of GOD—*this* is what it means to be Israel." This command, to give thanks, runs right down the center of all Christian worship. A decree. A word telling us what we ought to do, and that what we ought to do is praise.

When we sin and mess up our lives, we find that God doesn't go off and leave us—he enters into our trouble and saves us. That is good, an instance of what the Bible calls gospel. We discover reasons and motivations for living in faith and find that God is already helping us to do it—and that is good. Praise God! "A Christian," wrote Augustine, "should be an alleluia from head to foot." That is the reality. That is the truth of our lives. God made us, redeems us, provides for us. The natural, honest, healthy, logical response to that is praise to God. When we praise we are functioning at the center, we are in touch with the basic, core reality of our being.

But very often we don't feel like it, and so we say, "It would be dishonest for me to go to a place of worship and praise God when I don't feel like it. I would be a hypocrite." The psalm says, I don't care whether you feel like it or not: as was *decreed* (RSV), "give thanks to the name of GOD."

I have put great emphasis on the fact that Christians worship because they want to, not because they are forced to. But I have never said that we worship because we *feel* like it. Feelings are great liars. If Christians worshiped only when they felt like it, there would be precious little worship. Feelings are important in many areas but completely unreliable in matters of faith. Paul Scherer is laconic: "The Bible wastes very little time on the way we feel."[1]

We live in what one writer has called the "age of sensation."[2] We think that if we don't *feel* something there can be no authenticity in *doing* it. But the wisdom of God says something different: that we can *act* ourselves into a new way of feeling much quicker than we can *feel* ourselves into a new way of acting. Worship is an *act* that develops feelings for God, not a *feeling* for God that is expressed in an act of worship. When we obey the command to praise God in worship, our deep, essential need to be in relationship with God is nurtured.

A Word of God

A third reason we keep engaging in regular acts of worship is that in it our attention is centered on the decisions of God. Our psalm describes worship as the place where "thrones for righteous judgment are set . . . famous David-thrones." The biblical word *judgment* means "the decisive word by which God straightens things out and puts things right." Thrones of judgment are the places that word is announced. Judgment is not a word *about* things, describing them; it is a word that *does* things, putting love in motion, applying mercy, nullifying wrong, ordering goodness.

This word of God is everywhere in worship. In the call to worship we hear God's first word to us; in the benediction we hear God's last word to us; in the Scripture lessons we hear God speaking to our faith-parents; in the sermon we hear that word reexpressed to us; in the hymns, which are all to a greater or lesser extent paraphrases of Scripture, the Word of God makes our prayers articulate. Every time we worship our minds are informed, our memories refreshed with the judgments of God, we are familiarized with what God says, what he has decided, the ways he is working out our salvation.

There is simply no place where these can be done as well as in worship. If we stay at home by ourselves and read the Bible, we are going to miss a lot, for our reading will be unconsciously conditioned by our culture, limited by our ignorance, distorted by unnoticed prejudices. In worship we are part of "the large congregation" where all the writers of Scripture address us, where hymn writers use music to express truths that touch us not only in our heads but in our hearts, where the preacher who has just lived through six days of doubt, hurt, faith and blessing with the worshipers speaks the truth of Scripture in the language of the congregation's present experience. We want to hear what God says and what he says to us: worship is the place where our attention is centered on these personal and decisive words of God.

Peace and Security

Worship, even for those who are most faithful at it, takes up just a small percentage of a person's life, an hour or so a week at

most. Does it make any difference to the rest of the week? The
final words of Psalm 122 say that it does: "Pray for Jerusalem's
peace! Prosperity to all you Jerusalem-lovers! Friendly insiders,
get along! Hostile outsiders, keep your distance! For the sake of
my family and friends, I say it again: live in peace! For the sake
of the house of our God, GOD, I'll do my very best for you."
Here we have prayers that overflow the bounds of worship and
create new relationships in the city, in society.

The first word, *pray*, is a transition into the everyday world. It
is not the word ordinarily used in formal worship, but the everyday Hebrew word for "ask." It is not improperly translated
"pray," for when we ask from God we pray. But the asking is not
a formal prayer in the sanctuary; it is an informal asking as we go
about our business between Sundays. It is the word Hebrews
would use to ask for a second helping of bread if still hungry, or
for directions if lost.

Worship does not satisfy our hunger for God—it whets our
appetite. Our need for God is not taken care of by engaging in
worship—it deepens. It overflows the hour and permeates the
week. The need is expressed in a desire for peace and security.
Our everyday needs are changed by the act of worship. We are
no longer living from hand to mouth, greedily scrambling
through the human rat race to make the best we can out of a
mean existence. Our basic needs suddenly become worthy of the
dignity of creatures made in the image of God: peace and security. The words *shalom* and *shalvah* play on the sounds in Jerusalem, *yerushalayim*, the place of worship.

Shalom, "peace," is one of the richest words in the Bible. You
can no more define it by looking up its meaning in the dictionary than you can define a person by his or her social security
number. It gathers all aspects of wholeness that result from
God's will being completed in us. It is the work of God that,

when complete, releases streams of living water in us and pulsates with eternal life. Every time Jesus healed, forgave or called someone, we have a demonstration of *shalom*.

And *shalvah*, "prosperity." It has nothing to do with insurance policies or large bank accounts or stockpiles of weapons. The root meaning is leisure—the relaxed stance of one who knows that everything is all right because God is over us, with us and for us in Jesus Christ. It is the security of being at home in a history that has a cross at its center. It is the leisure of the person who knows that every moment of our existence is at the disposal of God, lived under the mercy of God.

Worship initiates an extended, daily participation in peace and prosperity so that we share in our daily rounds what God initiates and continues in Jesus Christ.

A Pause to Sharpen a Tool

We live in a pragmatic age and are reluctant to do anything if its practical usefulness cannot be demonstrated. It is inevitable that we ask regarding worship, is it worth it? Can you justify the time and energy and expense involved in gathering Christians together in worship? Well,

> look at the mower in the summer's day, with so much to cut down ere the sun sets. He pauses in his labour—is he a sluggard? He looks for his stone, and begins to draw it up and down his scythe, with rink-atink, rink-atink, rink-atink. Is that idle music— is he wasting precious moments? How much he might have mowed while he has been ringing out those notes on his scythe! But he is sharpening his tool, and he will do far more when once again he gives his strength to those long sweeps which lay the grass prostrate in rows before him.[3]

5

SERVICE

"Like Servants . . .
We're Watching & Waiting"

I look to you, heaven-dwelling God,
look up to you for help.
Like servants, alert to their master's commands,
like a maiden attending her lady,
We're watching and waiting, holding our breath,
awaiting your word of mercy.
Mercy, GOD, mercy!
We've been kicked around long enough,
Kicked in the teeth by complacent rich men,
kicked when we're down by arrogant brutes.

PSALM 123

In general terms, service is a willing, working, and doing in which a person acts not according to his own purposes or plans but with a view to the purpose of another person and according to the need, disposition, and direction of others.
It is an act whose freedom is limited and determined by the other's freedom, an act whose glory becomes increasingly greater to the extent that the doer is not concerned about his own glory but about the glory of the other. . . . It is ministerium Verbi divini, *which means, literally, "a servant's attendance on the divine Word." The expression "attendance" may call to mind the fact that the New Testament concept of* Diakonos *originally meant "a waiter." [We] must wait upon the high majesty of the divine Word, which is God himself as he speaks in his action.*

KARL BARTH

A s a person grows and matures in the Christian way, it is necessary to acquire certain skills. One is service. The skill is so difficult to acquire and liable to so many misunderstandings that it is necessary to single it out for special attention from time to time.

Psalm 123 is an instance of service. In this, as so often in the psalms, we are not instructed in what to do, we are provided an instance of what is done. A psalm is not a lecture; it is a song. In a psalm we have the observable evidence of what happens when a person of faith goes about the business of believing and loving and following God. We don't have a rule book defining the action, we have a snapshot of players playing the game. In Psalm 123 we observe that aspect of the life of discipleship that takes place under the form of servanthood.

If God Is God at All

"I look to you, heaven-dwelling God, look up to you for help." Service begins with an upward look to God. God is over us. He is above us. The person of faith looks up to God, not at him or down on him. The servant assumes a certain posture, a stance. If he or she fails to take that posture, attentive responsiveness to the master's commands will be hard.

It is easy to get the wrong idea, for when a person becomes a Christian there is a new sense of confident ability and assured power. Furthermore we are provided promises that tell us to go ahead:

Ask and you'll get;

Seek and you'll find;

Knock and the door will open. (Lk 11:9)

God presents himself to us in the history of Jesus Christ as a servant: with that before us it is easy to assume the role of master and begin ordering him around. But God is not a servant to be called into action when we are too tired to do something ourselves, not an expert to be called on when we find we are ill equipped to handle a specialized problem in living. Paul Scherer writes scathingly of people who lobby around in the courts of the Almighty for special favors, plucking at his sleeve, pestering him with requests. God is not a buddy we occasionally ask to join us at our convenience or for our diversion. God did not become a servant so that we could order him around but so that we could join him in a redemptive life.

Too often we think of religion as a far-off, mysteriously run bureaucracy to which we apply for assistance when we feel the need. We go to a local branch office and direct the clerk (sometimes called a pastor) to fill out our order for God. Then we go home and wait for God to be delivered to us according to the specifications that we have set down. But that is not the way it works. And if we thought about it for two consecutive minutes, we would not want it to work that way. If God is God at all, he must know more about our needs than we do; if God is God at all, he must be more in touch with the reality of our thoughts, our emotions, our bodies than we are; if God is God at all, he must have a more comprehensive grasp of the interrelations in our families and communities and nations than we do.

"Heaven-dwelling God." When the Bible uses that phrase, and it does use it frequently, it is not saying anything about geography or space. Biblical writers are neither geographers nor astronomers—they are theologians. They describe with profound accuracy the relation between God and persons like you and me, a relationship between the Creator and the creature; they coordinate our knowledge of the God who loves us with our experience of being loved; they tell the story of the God who leads us through difficulties and document it with our experience of being guided. We are not presented with a functional god who will help us out of jams or an entertainment god who will lighten tedious hours. We are presented with the God of exodus and Easter, the God of Sinai and Calvary. If we want to understand God, we must do it on his terms. If we want to see God the way he really is, we must look to the place of authority—to Scripture and to Jesus Christ.

And do we really want it any other way? I don't think so. We would very soon become contemptuous of a god whom we could figure out like a puzzle or learn to use like a tool. No, if God is worth our attention at all, he must be a God we can look up to—a God we *must* look up to: "I look to you, heaven-dwelling God."

The moment we look up to God (and not over at him, or down on him) we are in the posture of servitude.

Mercy, GOD, Mercy!

A second element in service has to do with our expectation. What happens when we look up to God in faith? There is an awesome mystery in God that we can never completely penetrate. We cannot define God; we cannot package God. But that doesn't mean that we don't know anything about God. It doesn't mean that we are completely at sea with God, never knowing what to expect, nervously on edge all the time, wondering what he might do.

We know very well what to expect, and what we expect is mercy. Three times the expectation is articulated in Psalm 123:

"We're watching and waiting, holding our breath, awaiting your word of mercy. Mercy, GOD, mercy!"

The basic conviction of a Christian is that God intends good for us and that he will get his way in us. He does not treat us according to our deserts, but according to his plan. He is not a police officer on patrol, watching over the universe, ready to club us if we get out of hand or put us in jail if we get obstreperous. He is a potter working with the clay of our lives, forming and reforming until, finally, he has shaped a redeemed life, a vessel fit for the kingdom.

"Mercy, GOD, mercy!": the prayer is not an attempt to get God to do what he is unwilling otherwise to do, but a reaching out to what we know that he does do, an expressed longing to receive what God is doing in and for us in Jesus Christ. In obedience we pray *"Mercy!"* instead of "Give us what we want." We pray *"Mercy!"* and not "Reward us for our goodness so our neighbors will acknowledge our superiority." We pray *"Mercy!"* and not "Punish us for our badness so we will feel better." We pray *"Mercy!"* and not "Be nice to us because we have been such good people."

We live under the mercy. God does not treat us as alien others, lining us up so that he can evaluate our competence or our usefulness or our worth. He rules, guides, commands, loves us as children whose destinies he carries in his heart.

The word *mercy* means that the upward look to God in the heavens does not expect God to stay in the heavens but to come down, to enter our condition, to accomplish the vast enterprise of redemption, to fashion in us his eternal salvation. "The root meaning 'to stoop,' 'to be inclined,' has been conjectured."[1] Servitude is not a vague woolgathering in the general direction of God and certainly not a cringing, cowering terror under the lash of God. Servitude is specific in its expectation, and what it expects is mercy.

Urgent Service

A third element in the servant life is urgency: "Mercy. . . . We've been kicked around long enough, / Kicked in the teeth by complacent rich men, / kicked when we're down by arrogant brutes."

The experience of servitude is recurrent through history. And the experience has never been happy. The psalmist lived in a culture in which the slave and the servant were institutionalized, as they have been at different times in world history. As far as we can tell, it has never worked very well. Power breeds oppression. Masters get lazy and become scornful of those under them. The cry "We've been kicked around long enough, kicked in the teeth . . . kicked when we're down" is believable. The psalm is part of a vast literature of outcry, a longing for deliverance from oppression.

We live in a similar slavery. True, we have, in Western countries, abolished the institutionalized forms of slavery and all but eliminated a servant class, but the experience of servitude is still among us and is as oppressive as ever. Freedom is on everyone's lips. Freedom is announced and celebrated. But not many feel or act free. Evidence? We live in a nation of complainers and a society of addicts. Everywhere we turn we hear complaints: I can't spend my money the way I want; I can't spend my time the way I want; I can't be myself; I'm under the control of others all the time. And everywhere we meet the addicts—addiction to alcohol and drugs, to compulsive work habits and to obsessive consumption. We trade masters; we stay enslaved.

The Christian is a person who recognizes that our real problem is not in achieving freedom but in learning service under a better master. The Christian realizes that every relationship that excludes God becomes oppressive. Recognizing and realizing that, we urgently want to live under the mastery of God.

For such reasons all Christian service involves urgency. Servitude is not a casual standing around waiting for orders. It is never desultory; it is urgent need: "Speak, Lord, for thy servant heareth." And the gospel is the good news that the words of God, commanding new life in us, are already in our ears; "those who have ears to hear, let them hear."

Reasonable Service

The best New Testament commentary on this psalm is in the final section of Paul's letter to the Romans, chapters 12—16. The section begins with this sentence: "So here's what I want you to do, God helping you: Take your everyday, ordinary life—your sleeping, eating, going-to-work, and walking-around life—and place it before God as an offering" (12:1). The psalm's emphasis on actual, physical service (not a spiritual intention, not a desire to be of service) is picked up in the invitation to present our *everyday, ordinary life*. The motivation for service (not coerced, not demanded) is picked up in the phrase "God helping you." But most significant is the remarkable last phrase *logikēn latreian,* "place it before God as an offering," which another translation renders "reasonable service." Service, that is, that makes sense. The word *latreia* means "service," the work one does on behalf of the community. But it also is the base of our word *liturgy,* the service of worship that we render to God. And it is precisely that service that is logical, reasonable. The service we offer to God (in worship) is extended into specific acts that serve others. We learn a relationship—an attitude toward life, a stance—of servitude before God, and then we are available to be of use to others in acts of service.

The psalm has nothing in it about serving others. It concentrates on being a servant to God. Its position is that if the attitude of servanthood is learned, by attending to God as Lord, then serving others will develop as a very natural way of life. Commands will be heard to be hospitable, to be compassionate, to visit the sick, to help and to heal (commands that Paul assembles in Romans 12—16 and many other places) and carried out with ease and poise.

As we live out the implications of a life of service, we are provided with continuous encouragement and example by Jesus Christ, who said:

> Do you understand what I have done to you? You address me as "Teacher" and "Master," and rightly so. That is what I am. So if I, the Master and Teacher, washed your feet, you must now wash each other's feet. I've laid down a pattern for you. What I've done, you do. I'm only pointing out the obvious. A servant is not ranked above his master; an employee doesn't give orders to the employer. If you understand what I'm telling you, act like it—and live a blessed life. (Jn 13:12-17)

The Freest Person on Earth

God's people are everywhere and always encouraged to work for the liberation of others, helping to free them from every form of bondage—religious, economic, cultural, political—that sin uses to stunt or thwart or cramp their lives. The promises and fulfillments of freedom are antiphonal throughout Scripture. The glorious theme has extensive documentation in the lives of the people of God. But there are also, sadly, numerous instances in our society of persons who, having been given their freedom, have at once squandered it, using it as "an excuse to do whatever you want" (Gal 5:13), ending in a worse slavery. For freedom is the freedom to live as persons in love for the sake of God and neighbor, not a license to grab and push. It is the opportunity to live at our best, "little less than God" (Ps 8:5 RSV), not as unruly beasts. The work of liberation must therefore be accompanied by instruction in the use of liberty as children of God who "walk by the Spirit" (Gal 5:25 RSV).

Those who parade the rhetoric of liberation but scorn the wisdom of service do not lead people into the glorious liberty of the children of God but into a cramped and covetous squalor.

As Psalm 123 prays the transition from oppression ("kicked in the teeth by complacent rich men") to freedom ("awaiting your word of mercy") to a new servitude ("like servants, alert to their master's commands"), it puts us in the way of learning how to use our freedom most appropriately, under the lordship of a merciful God. The consequences are all positive. I have never yet heard a servant Christian complain of the oppressiveness of his servitude. I have never yet heard a servant Christian rail against the restrictions of her service. A servant Christian is the freest person on earth.

6

HELP

"Oh, Blessed Be GOD!
He Didn't Go Off & Leave Us"

If GOD hadn't been for us
—all together now, Israel, sing out!—
If GOD hadn't been for us
when everyone went against us,
We would have been swallowed alive
by their violent anger,
Swept away by the flood of rage,
drowned in the torrent;
We would have lost our lives
in the wild, raging water.
Oh, blessed be GOD!
He didn't go off and leave us.
He didn't abandon us defenseless,
helpless as a rabbit in a pack of snarling dogs.
We've flown free from their fangs,
free of their traps, free as a bird.
Their grip is broken;
we're free as a bird in flight.
GOD's strong name is our help,
the same GOD who made heaven and earth.

PSALM 124

God is almost intolerably careless about crosses and swords,
arenas and scaffolds, about all the "evils" and all the "plagues."
His caring doesn't mean that he goes in for upholstering!

PAUL SCHERER

I was at a Red Cross bloodmobile to donate my annual pint, and a nurse asked me a series of questions to see if there was any reason for disqualification. The final question on the list was "Do you engage in hazardous work?" I said, "Yes."

Her routine was interrupted: she looked up, a little surprised, for I was wearing a clerical collar by which she could identify me as a pastor. Her hesitation was only momentary: she smiled, ignored my answer and marked no on her questionnaire, saying, "I don't mean *that* kind of hazardous."

I would have liked to continue the conversation, comparing what she supposed I meant by hazardous with what I did in fact mean by it. But that was not the appropriate time and place. There was a line of people waiting for their turn at the needle.

There are, though, appropriate times and places for just such conversations, and one of them is when Christians encounter Psalm 124. Psalm 124 is a song of hazard—and of help. Among the Songs of Ascents, sung by the people of God on the way of faith, this is one that better than any other describes the hazardous work of all discipleship and declares the help that is always experienced at the hand of God.

A Clerk in the Complaints Department of Humanity

The first lines of the psalm twice describe God as "for us." The last line is "GOD's strong name is our help, the same GOD who made heaven and earth." God is for us. God is our help.

For some people, statements like that are red flags. They provoke challenges. I, confident and assured in the pulpit, can announce, "The Lord is for us. . . . God's strong name is our help." But no sooner am I out of the pulpit than someone is saying to me, "Look, I wish you would be a little more careful about your pronouns. How do you get this *our*? The Lord might be for *you*, he might be *your* help. But he is not mine. Listen to this . . ." Through the week I get case histories of family tragedy and career disappointment, along with pessimistic recountings of world events. The concluding line is a variation on the theme: "How do you explain that, you who are so sure that God is for me?"

I am put on the spot of being God's defender. I am expected to explain God to his disappointed clients. I am thrust into the role of a clerk in the complaints department of humanity, asked to trace down bad service, listen sympathetically to aggrieved patrons, try to put right any mistakes I can and apologize for the rudeness of the management.

But if I accept any of these assignments I misunderstand my proper work, for God doesn't need me to defend him. He doesn't need me for a press secretary, explaining to the world that he didn't really say what everyone thought they heard in that interview with Job, or that the quotation of his word by St. Paul was taken out of context and needs to be understood against the background paper that Isaiah wrote.

The proper work for the Christian is witness, not apology, and Psalm 124 is an excellent model. It does not argue God's help; it does not explain God's help; it is a testimony of God's help in the form of a song. The song is so vigorous, so confident, so bursting with what can only be called reality that it fundamentally changes our approach and our questions. No longer does it seem of the highest priority to ask, "Why did this happen to me? Why do I feel left in the lurch?" Instead we ask, "How does it happen that there are people who sing with such confidence, 'God's strong name is our help'?" The psalm is data that must be accounted for, and the data are so solid, so vital, have so much more substance and are so much more interesting than the other things we hear through the day that it must be dealt with before we can go back to the whimpering complaints.

> If GOD hadn't been for us
> —all together now, Israel, sing out!—
> If GOD hadn't been for us
> when everyone went against us,
> We would have been swallowed alive
> by their violent anger,
> Swept away by the flood of rage,
> drowned in the torrent;
> We would have lost our lives
> in the wild, raging water.

The witness is vivid and contagious. One person announces the theme, everyone joins in. God's help is not a private experience; it is a corporate reality—not an exception that occurs among isolated strangers, but the norm among the people of God.

God's help is described by means of two illustrations. The people were in danger of being swallowed up alive; and they were in danger of being drowned by a flood. The first picture is of an enormous dragon or sea monster. Nobody has ever seen a dragon, but everybody (especially children) knows they exist. Dragons are projections of our fears, horrible constructions of all that might hurt us. A dragon is total evil. A peasant confronted by a magnificent dragon is completely outclassed. There is no escape: the dragon's thick skin, fiery mouth, lashing serpentine tail, and insatiable greed and lust sign an immediate doom.

The second picture, the flood, speaks of sudden disaster. In the Middle East, watercourses that have eroded the countryside are all interconnected by an intricate gravitational system. A sudden storm fills these little gullies with water, they feed into one another, and in a very few minutes a torrential flash flood is produced. During the rainy season, such unannounced catastrophes pose great danger for persons who live in these desert areas. There is no escaping. One minute you are well and happy and making plans for the future; the next minute the entire world is disarranged by a catastrophe.

The psalmist is not a person talking about the good life, how God has kept him out of all difficulty. This person has gone through the worst—the dragon's mouth, the flood's torrent—and finds himself intact. He was not abandoned but helped. The final strength is not in the dragon or in the flood but in God who "didn't go off and leave us."

We can, of course, avoid dealing with this by employing a cheap back-of-the-hand cynicism. It is inevitable, in one sense, that we should respond to enthusiasm with some cynicism. Advertisers are routinely so dishonest with us that we train ourselves to keep our distance from any who speak with passion and excitement for fear they will manipulate us. We see Michael Jordan or Tiger Woods or Martha Stewart speaking on behalf of a product and inwardly discount the witness; we know the words were written by a highly paid copywriter and that the testimonial was done for a handsome fee. In the midst of that kind of world we come on the lines "If God hadn't been for us when everyone went against us, / We would have been swallowed alive," and we say, "Vigorous poetry! Well done! But who was your copywriter, and how much did they pay you to say it?"

The only cure for that kind of cynicism is to bring it out in the open and deal with it. If it is left to work behind the scenes in our hearts, it is a parasite on faith, enervates hope and leaves us anemic in love. Don't hesitate to put the psalm (or any other Scripture passage) under the searchlight of your disbelief! The reason many of us do not ardently believe in the gospel is that we have never given it a rigorous testing, thrown our hard questions at it, faced it with our most prickly doubts.

Subjected to our most relentless and searching criticism, Psalm 124 will, I think, finally convince us of its honesty. There is no literature in all the world that is more true to life and more honest than Psalms, for here we have warts-and-all religion. Every skeptical thought, every disappointing venture, every pain, every despair that we can face is lived through and integrated into a personal, saving relationship with God—a relationship that also has in it acts of praise, blessing, peace, security, trust and love.

Good poetry survives not when it is pretty or beautiful or nice but when it is true: accurate and honest. The psalms are great poetry and have lasted not because they appeal to our fantasies and our wishes but because they are confirmed in the intensities of honest and hazardous living. Psalm 124 is not a selected witness, inserted like a commercial into our lives to testify that life goes better with God; it is not part of a media blitz to convince us that God is superior to all the other gods on the market. It is not a press release. It is honest prayer.

The people who know this psalm best and who have tested it out and used it often (that is, the people of God who are travelers on the way of faith, singing it in all kinds of weather) tell us that it is credible, that it fits into what we know of life lived in faith.

Hazardous Work

Christian discipleship is hazardous work. I hope the Red Cross nurse did not think that I was referring to my pastoral work as hazardous. My work, as such, is no more difficult than anyone else's. Any work done faithfully and well is difficult. It is no harder for me to do my job well than for any other person, and no less. There are no easy tasks in the Christian way; there are only tasks that can be done faithfully or erratically, with joy or with resentment. And there is no room for any of us, pastors or grocers, accountants or engineers, word processors or gardeners, physicians or teamsters, to speak in tones of self-pity of the terrible burdens of our work.

What is hazardous in my life is my work as a Christian. Every day I put faith on the line. I have never seen God. In a world where nearly everything can be weighed, explained, quantified, subjected to psychological analysis and scientific control, I persist in making the center of my life a God whom no eye hath seen, nor ear heard, whose will no one can probe. That's a risk.

Every day I put hope on the line. I don't know one thing about the future. I don't know what the next hour will hold. There may be sickness, accident, personal or world catastrophe. Before this day is over I may have to deal with death, pain, loss, rejection. I don't know what the future holds for me, for those I love, for my nation, for this world. Still, despite my ignorance and surrounded by tinny optimists and cowardly pessimists, I say that God will accomplish his will, and I cheerfully persist in living in the hope that nothing will separate me from Christ's love.

Every day I put love on the line. There is nothing I am less good at than love. I am far better in competition than in love. I am far better at responding to my instincts and ambitions to get ahead and make my mark than I am at figuring out how to love another. I am schooled and trained in acquisitive skills, in getting my own way. And yet I decide, every day, to set aside what I

can do best and attempt what I do very clumsily—open myself
to the frustrations and failures of loving, daring to believe that
failing in love is better than succeeding in pride.

All that is hazardous work; I live on the edge of defeat all the
time. I have never done any one of those things to my (or anyone else's) satisfaction. I live in the dragon's maw and at the
flood's edge. "How very hard it is to be / A Christian. Hard for
you and me."[1]

The psalm, though, is not about hazards but about help. The
hazardous work of discipleship is not the subject of the psalm
but only its setting. The subject is help: "Oh, blessed be GOD!
. . . He didn't abandon us defenseless, helpless as a rabbit in a
pack of snarling dogs. We've flown free from their fangs, free of
their traps, . . . we're free as a bird in flight. GOD's strong name
is our help, the same GOD who made heaven and earth." Hazards or no hazards, the fundamental reality we live with is God
who is "for us . . . GOD's strong name is our help."

When we are first in danger, our consciousness of hazard is
total: like a bird trapped in a snare. All the facts add up to doom.
There is no way out. And then, unaccountably, there *is* a way
out. The snare breaks and the bird escapes. Deliverance is a surprise. Rescue is a miracle. "Oh, blessed be GOD! . . . He didn't
abandon us defenseless."

How God wants us to sing like this! Christians are not fussy
moralists who cluck their tongues over a world going to hell;
Christians are people who praise the God who is on our side.
Christians are not pious pretenders in the midst of a decadent
culture; Christians are robust witnesses to the God who is our
help. Christians are not fatigued outcasts who carry righteousness as a burden in a world where the wicked flourish; Christians
are people who sing "Oh, blessed be GOD! . . . He didn't abandon us defenseless."

Enlarged Photographs of Ordinary Objects

The final sentence, "GOD's strong name is our help, the same GOD who made heaven and earth," links the God who created heaven and earth to the God who helps us personally. It takes the majesty of the One who pulled a universe into order and beauty, and finds this same God involved in the local troubles of a quite ordinary person.

A friend showed me a series of pictures he had taken. The subject matter consisted exclusively of household items found in an ordinary kitchen: a matchstick, a pin, the edge of a knife. Household utensils are not ordinarily thought of as possessing much beauty, but all these photographs of very ordinary objects were quite astonishingly beautiful. The beauty was suddenly visible because the photographs had all been made through a magnifying lens. Small, ugly, insignificant items were blown up to great size, and we could see what we had overlooked in our everyday routine. And it turned out that what we had overlooked was careful, planned details that produced exquisite beauty.

I particularly remember the photograph of a highly magnified Brillo pad. Nothing in the kitchen seems quite as ordinary or quite as lacking in aesthetic appeal. When possible we keep Brillo pads hidden under the sink. No one would think of hanging one on a nail or hook for people to admire. Yet under magnification the Brillo pad is one of the most beautiful of kitchen items. The swirl of fine wire is pleasing to the eye. The colors of blue fade in and out of the soap film. What we assume is not worth looking at twice, and best kept in an obscure place, is, on examination, a beautiful construction.

Psalm 124 is a magnification of the items of life that are thought to be unpleasant, best kept under cover, best surrounded with silence lest they clutter our lives with unpleasantness: the dragon's mouth, the flood's torrent, the snare's entrapment; suffering, catastrophe, disaster. They are a very real part of life, and they constitute a dominating, fearful background for many. We look for relief among experts in medicine and psychology; we go to museums to get a look at beauty. Psalm 124 is an instance of a person who digs deeply into the trouble and finds there the presence of the God who is on our side. In the details of the conflict, in the minuteness of a personal history, the majestic greatness of God becomes revealed. Faith develops out of the most difficult aspects of our existence, not the easiest.

The person of faith is not a person who has been born, luckily, with a good digestion and sunny disposition. The assumption by outsiders that Christians are naive or protected is the opposite of the truth: Christians know more about the deep struggles of life than others, more about the ugliness of sin.

A look to the heavens can bring a breathtaking sense of wonder and majesty and, if a person is a believer, a feeling of praise to the God who made heaven and earth. This psalm looks the other direction. It looks into the troubles of history, the anxiety of personal conflict and emotional trauma. And it sees there the God who is on our side, God our help. The close look, the microscopic insight into the dragon's terrors, the flood's waters and the imprisoning trap, sees the action of God in deliverance.

We speak our words of praise in a world that is hellish; we sing our songs of victory in a world where things get messy; we live our joy among people who neither understand nor encourage us. But the content of our lives is God, not humanity. We are not scavenging in the dark alleys of the world, poking in its garbage cans for a bare subsistence. We are traveling in the light, toward God who is rich in mercy and strong to save. It is Christ, not culture, that defines our lives. It is the help we experience, not the hazards we risk, that shapes our days.

7

SECURITY

"GOD Encircles His People"

Those who trust in GOD
are like Zion Mountain:
Nothing can move it, a rock-solid mountain
you can always depend on.
Mountains encircle Jerusalem,
and GOD encircles his people—
always has and always will.
The fist of the wicked
will never violate
What is due the righteous,
provoking wrongful violence.
Be good to your good people, GOD,
to those whose hearts are right!
GOD will round up the backsliders,
corral them with the incorrigibles.
Peace over Israel!

PSALM 125

Judea was designed to produce in her inhabitants the sense of seclusion and security, though not to such a degree as to relieve them from the attractions of the great world, which throbbed closely past, or to relax in them those habits of discipline, vigilance, and valour, which are the necessary elements of a nation's character. In the position of Judea there was not enough to tempt her people to put their confidence in herself, but there was enough to encourage them to defend their freedom and a strenuous life. And while the isolation of their land was sufficient to confirm their calling to a discipline and destiny separate from other peoples, it was not so complete as to keep them in ignorance of the world or to release them from those temptations to mix with the world, in combating which their discipline and destiny could alone be realised.

GEORGE ADAM SMITH

C limbing is difficult. The tug of gravity is constant. There are barriers to be surmounted and hazards to be met. Ordinarily, though, with a moderate amount of determination and stamina, people complete the climb they begin. But sometimes the foothold gives way and there is a slide backward.

The Rocky Mountains, where our family loves to hike, are mostly sedimentary rock. There are places where the rock, under the impact of ice and water, erodes to a loose, crumbly stuff called scree. A misstep there can send you cascading down a mountain slope for hundreds of feet.

Backslider was a basic word in the religious vocabulary I learned as I grew up. *Exempla* were on display throughout the town: people who had made a commitment of faith to our Lord, had been active in our little church but had lost their footing on the ascent to Christ and backslid. My uncle Oscar was a backslider. He had been a warm, ardent Christian. In his middle years, on the basis of a mere wisp of rumor, he acquired hundreds of acres of useless land. Not long afterward the Department of the Interior decided to build a hydroelectric dam on that land. Suddenly my uncle was a rich man. The excitement of making money got into his blood; attendance at worship became infrequent. He became impatient with his children and with me, his nephew. His work habits became compulsive. That was when I first heard *backslider* applied to someone I knew. He died of high blood pressure and a heart attack. Everyone in his family visibly relaxed.

Two girls, older than I, whom I very much admired, attractive and vivacious, went away to college. They returned for vacation wearing brighter lipstick and shorter skirts. From the pew in front of me on a Sunday morning I heard the stage whispers between two grandmotherly types: "Do you think they have backslidden?" One became a pastor's wife, the other a missionary with her husband in Africa.

Backsliding was everywhere and always an ominous possibility. Warnings were frequent and the sad consequences on public display. The mood was anxious and worried. I was taught to take my spiritual temperature every day, or at least every week; if it was not exactly "normal," there was general panic. I got the feeling that backsliding was not something you *did*, it happened to you. It was an accident that intruded on the unwary or an attack that involved the undefended.

Later in life, as I read Scripture for myself, and still later when as a pastor I had the responsibility for guiding the spiritual development of others, I acquired a very different way of looking at the conditions under which the Christian walks the way of discipleship. In both the Scriptures and the pastoral traditions of the church I found a background of confidence, a leisured security, among persons of faith.

Someone Else Built the Fortress

The emphasis of Psalm 125 is not on the precariousness of the Christian life but on its solidity. Living as a Christian is not walking a tightrope without a safety net high above a breathless crowd, many of whom would like nothing better than the morbid thrill of seeing you fall; it is sitting secure in a fortress.

The psalm uses familiar geography to demonstrate the truth:

Those who trust in GOD
   are like Zion Mountain:
Nothing can move it, a rock-solid mountain
   you can always depend on.
Mountains encircle Jerusalem,
   and GOD encircles his people—
   always has and always will.

Jerusalem was set in a saucer of hills. It was the safest of cities because of the protective fortress these hills provided. Just so is the person of faith surrounded by the Lord. Better than a city wall, better than a military fortification is the presence of the God of peace. Geographically the city of Jerusalem had "borders and bulwarks of extraordinary variety and intricacy"[1] which illustrated and enforced the reality of God's secure love and care.

City life in the ancient world was dangerous. The outside world was filled with roaming marauders, ready to attack at any sign of weakness. Constant vigilance was a prerequisite for community life and for the development of the arts of civilization. Cities needed elaborate and extensive defense systems to make them safe. Immense effort was expended on building walls and digging moats.

We still live in that kind of world, and we still build those defenses although the forms have changed somewhat. The process is not only political but personal. The outer world is only an extension of an inner, spiritual world. Psychologists who observe us talk of the elaborate security systems (Sullivan) and the defense mechanisms (Freud) that we use to protect ourselves.

People of faith have the same needs for protection and security as anyone else. We are no better than others in that regard. What is different is that we find that we don't have to build our own: "God is a safe place to hide, ready to help when we need him" (Ps 46:1). "Mountains encircle Jerusalem, and GOD encircles his people." We don't always have to be looking over our shoulder lest evil overtake us unawares. We don't always have to keep our eyes on our footsteps lest we slip, inadvertently, on a temptation. God is at our side. He is, as another psalmist put it, "behind and before" (see 139:5). And when it comes down to it, do we need anything more than our Lord's prayer for us: "Holy Father, guard them. . . . I'm not asking that you take them out of the world / But that you guard them from the Evil One" (Jn 17:11, 15)? With a prayer like that offered to the Father on our behalf, are we not secure?

A Saw-Toothed History

All the same, we do become anxious, we do slip into fearful moods, we become uncertain and insecure. The confident, robust faith that we desire and think is our destiny is qualified by recurrent insecurities. Singing Psalm 125 is one way Christians have to develop confidence and banish insecurity. The psalm makes its mark not by naively whistling when life is dark but by honestly facing the typical insecurities that beset us and putting them in their place.

One threat to our security comes from feelings of depression and doubt. The person of faith is described in this psalm as "a rock-solid mountain . . . nothing can move it." But I *am* moved. I am full of faith one day and empty with doubt the next. I wake up one morning full of vitality, rejoicing in the sun; the next day I am gray and dismal, faltering and moody. "Nothing can move it"?—nothing could be less true of me. I can be moved by nearly anything: sadness, joy, success, failure. I'm a thermometer and go up and down with the weather.

A couple of years ago a friend introduced me to the phrase "the saw-toothed history of Israel." Israel was up one day and down the next. One day they were marching in triumph through the Red Sea, singing songs of victory, the next they were grumbling in the desert because they missed having Egyptian steak and potatoes for supper. One day they were marching around Jericho blowing trumpets and raising hearty hymns, and the next they were plunged into an orgy at some Canaanite fertility shrine. One day they are with Jesus in the upper room, listening in rapt attention to his commands and receiving his love, the next they are stomping around and cursing in the courtyard, denying they ever knew him.

But all the time, as we read that saw-toothed history, we realize something solid and steady: they are always God's people. God is steadfastly with them, in mercy and judgment, insistently gracious. We get the feeling that everything is done in the sure, certain environment of the God who redeems his people. And as we learn that, we learn to live not by our feelings about God but by the facts of God. I refuse to believe my depressions; I choose to believe in God. If I break my leg I do not become less a person. My wife and children do not repudiate me. Neither when my faith fractures or my feelings bruise does God cast me off and reject me.

My feelings are important for many things. They are essential and valuable. They keep me aware of much that is true and real. But they tell me next to nothing about God or my relation to God. My security comes from who God is, not from how I feel. Discipleship is a decision to live by what I know about God, not by what I *feel* about him or myself or my neighbors. "As the mountains are round about Jerusalem, so the LORD is round about his people." The image that announces the dependable, unchanging, safe, secure existence of God's people comes from geology, not psychology.

A Damoclean Sword
Another source of uncertainty is our pain and suffering.

Unpleasant things happen to us. We lose what we think we cannot live without. Pain comes to those we love, and we conclude that there is no justice. Why does God permit this? Anxiety seeps into our hearts. We have the precarious feeling of living under a Damoclean sword. When will the ax fall on me? If such a terrible thing could happen to my friend who is so good, how long until I get mine?

The psalmist knows all this. Sickness and death, despair and persecution. He is familiar with the rape and pillage of military invasion and the famine and earthquake of natural disaster. Psalm 125 was written by a person who did not have anesthetics in his hospital or aspirin in his medicine chest and whose government did not have hundreds of billions of dollars to spend on national defense. Pain and suffering were most certainly part of his daily life. Why did they not destroy his confidence?

The answer is in these words: "The fist of the wicked / will never violate / What is due the righteous, / provoking wrongful violence." The key word is *violate:* cancel GOD's purposes that are being worked out. Israel had more than its share of oppression. The fist of the wicked was on Israel time and time again: Pharaoh, the Philistines, Tiglath-Pileser, Sennacherib, Nebuchadnezzar, Caesar. To an outsider it must have looked much of the time as if the wicked fist dominated the Israelites' lives. From the inside the witness of faith said that it did not: "The fist of the wicked / will never violate / What is due the righteous, / provoking wrongful violence."

If the evil fist is permanent, if there is no hope for salvation, even the most faithful and devout person will break and respond in "wrongful violence." But God does not permit that to happen. Danger and oppression are never too much for faith. They were not too much for Job, they were not too much for Jeremiah, and they were not too much for Jesus. Evil is always temporary. "The worst does not last."[2] Nothing counter to God's justice has any eternity to it. Paul's witness was "No test or temptation that comes your way is beyond the course of what others have had to face. All you need to remember is that God will never let you down; he'll never let you be pushed past your limit; he'll always be there to help you come through it" (1 Cor 10:13). "He knows when to say, It is enough."[3]

A Nonnegotiable Contract

The third threat to the confidence promised to the Christian is the known possibility of defection. The general truth under which the Christian lives in this regard is "once saved always saved." Once you are a Christian there is no getting out of it. It is a nonnegotiable contract. Once you have signed you cannot become a free agent again, no matter what the commissioner or the Supreme Court rules.

However true that is generally, and I think it is, there are exceptions. It would seem that if God will not force us to faith in the first place, he will not keep us against our will finally. Falling away is possible. We know of Judas. We know of Hymenaeus and Alexander, who "made shipwreck of their faith" (see 1 Tim 1:19-20). These are the ones described in the psalm as "the backsliders."[4] The way of discipleship gets difficult; they see an opening through the trees that promises a softer, easier path. Distracted and diverted, they slip off and never return.

If it is possible to defect, how do I know that I won't—or even worse, that I haven't? How do I know that I have not already lost faith, especially during times when I am depressed or have one calamity after another piled on me?

Such insinuated insecurities need to be confronted directly and plainly. It is not possible to drift unconsciously from faith to perdition. We wander like lost sheep, true; but God is a faithful shepherd who pursues us relentlessly. We have our ups and downs, zealously believing one day and gloomily doubting the next, but he is faithful. We break our promises, but he doesn't break his. Discipleship is not a contract in which if we break our part of the agreement he is free to break his; it is a covenant in which he establishes the conditions and guarantees the results.

Certainly you may quit if you wish. You may say no to God. It's a free faith. You may choose the crooked way. He will not keep you against your will. But it is not the kind of thing you fall into by chance or slip into by ignorance. Defection requires a deliberate, sustained and determined act of rejection.

All the persons of faith I know are sinners, doubters, uneven performers. We are secure not because we are sure of ourselves but because we trust that God is sure of us. The opening phrase of the psalm is "those who trust in GOD"—not those who trust in their performance, in their morals, in their righteousness, in their health, in their pastor, in their doctor, in their president, in their economy, in their nation—"those who trust in GOD." Those who decide that God is for us and will make us whole eternally.

Mountain Climbers Roped Together

When I was a child I walked about a mile to school each day with my two best friends. Along a quarter of that distance there was a railway track. When we came to that stretch we always walked on the rails. Each of us wanted to make it all the way without falling off, but didn't want the others to similarly succeed. We would throw things at each other to upset balance, or say things to divert attention, cry out that the train was coming or announce that there was a dead body in the ditch.

Some have supposed that that is what Christian living is, teetering and wobbling along a rail, taunted by the devil and his angels. With some skill and a lot of luck we might just make it to heaven, but it's an uncertain business at best.

Psalm 125 says that is not the way it is at all. Being a Christian is like sitting in the middle of Jerusalem, fortified and secure. "First we are established and then entrenched; settled, and then sentinelled: made like a mount, and then protected as if by mountains."[5] And so the last sentence is "Peace over Israel!" A colloquial, but in the context accurate, translation would be "Relax." We are secure. God is running the show. Neither our feelings of depression nor the facts of suffering nor the possibilities of defection are evidence that God has abandoned us. There is nothing more certain than that he will accomplish his salvation in our lives and perfect his will in our histories. Three times in his great Sermon, Jesus, knowing how easily we imagine the worst, repeats the reassuring command "Do not be anxious" (Mt 6:25, 31, 34 RSV). Our life with God is a sure thing.

When mountain climbers are in dangerous terrain, on the face of a cliff or the slopes of a glacier, they rope themselves together. Sometimes one of them slips and falls—backslides. But not everyone falls at once, and so those who are still on their feet are able to keep the backslider from falling away completely. And of course, in any group of climbers there is a veteran climber in the lead, identified for us in the letter to the Hebrews as "Jesus, who both began and finished this race we're in" (Heb 12:2).

Traveling in the way of faith and climbing the ascent to Christ may be difficult, but it is not worrisome. The weather may be adverse, but it is never fatal. We may slip and stumble and fall, but the rope will hold us.

8

JOY

"We Laughed, We Sang"

It seemed like a dream, too good to be true,
when GOD returned Zion's exiles.
We laughed, we sang,
we couldn't believe our good fortune.
We were the talk of the nations—
"GOD was wonderful to them!"
GOD was wonderful to us;
we are one happy people.
And now, GOD, do it again—
bring rains to our drought-stricken lives
So those who planted their crops in despair
will shout hurrahs at the harvest,
So those who went off with heavy hearts
will come home laughing, with armloads of blessing.

PSALM 126

*I have read that during the process of canonization
the Catholic Church demands proof of joy in the candidate,
and although I have not been able to track down chapter and verse
I like the suggestion that dourness is not a sacred attribute.*

PHYLLIS MCGINLEY

E llen Glasgow, in her autobiography, tells of her father who was a Presbyterian elder, full of rectitude and rigid with duty: "He was entirely unselfish, and in his long life he never committed a pleasure."[1] Peter Jay, in a political column in the *Baltimore Sun*, described the sober intensity and personal austerities of one of our Maryland politicians and then threw in this line: "He dresses like a Presbyterian."

I know there are Christians, so-called, who never crack a smile and who can't abide a joke, and I suppose Presbyterians contribute their quota. But I don't meet very many of them. The stereotype as such is a big lie created, presumably, by the devil. One of the delightful discoveries along the way of Christian discipleship is how much enjoyment there is, how much laughter you hear, how much sheer fun you find.

In Phyllis McGinley's delightful book *Saint-Watching* there is this story: "Martin Luther's close friend was Philipp Melanchthon, author of the Augsburg Confession. Melanchthon was a cool man where Luther was fervid, a scholar as opposed to a doer, and he continued to live like a monk even after he had joined the German Reformation. . . . One day Luther lost patience with Melanchthon's virtuous reserve. 'For heaven's sake,' he roared, 'why don't you go out and sin a little? God deserves to have something to forgive you for!' "[2]

A Consequence, Not a Requirement

"We laughed, we sang, we couldn't believe our good fortune."

That is the authentic Christian note, a sign of those who are on the way of salvation. Joy is characteristic of Christian pilgrimage. It is the second in Paul's list of the fruits of the Spirit (Gal 5:22-23). It is the first of Jesus' signs in the Gospel of John (turning water into wine). It was said of the Hasid Levi-Yitzhak of Berditchev: "His smiles were fraught with greater meaning than his sermons."[3] The same thing can be said of much of the Bible: its smiles carry more meaning than its sermons.

This is not to say that joy is a moral requirement for Christian living. Some of us experience events that are full of sadness and pain. Some of us descend to low points in our lives when joy seems to have permanently departed. We must not in such circumstances or during such times say, "Well, that's the final proof that I am not a good Christian. Christians are supposed to have their mouths filled with laughter and tongues with shouts of joy; and I don't. I'm not joyful, therefore I must not be a Christian."

Joy is not a requirement of Christian discipleship, it is a consequence. It is not what we have to acquire in order to experience life in Christ; it is what comes to us when we are walking in the way of faith and obedience.

We come to God (and to the revelation of God's ways) because none of us have it within ourselves, except momentarily, to be joyous. Joy is a product of abundance; it is the overflow of vitality. It is life working together harmoniously. It is exuberance. Inadequate sinners as we are, none of us can manage that for very long.

We try to get it through entertainment. We pay someone to make jokes, tell stories, perform dramatic actions, sing songs. We buy the vitality of another's imagination to divert and enliven our own poor lives. The enormous entertainment industry in America is a sign of the depletion of joy in our culture. Society is a bored, gluttonous king employing a court jester to divert

it after an overindulgent meal. But that kind of joy never penetrates our lives, never changes our basic constitution. The effects
are extremely temporary—a few minutes, a few hours, a few
days at most. When we run out of money, the joy trickles away.
We cannot make ourselves joyful. Joy cannot be commanded,
purchased or arranged.

But there is something we can do. We can decide to live in response to the abundance of God and not under the dictatorship
of our own poor needs. We can decide to live in the environment of a living God and not our own dying selves. We can decide to center ourselves in the God who generously gives and
not in our own egos which greedily grab. One of the certain
consequences of such a life is joy, the kind expressed in Psalm
126.

Joy: Past, Present, Future
The center sentence in the psalm is "We are one happy people"
(v. 3). The words on one side of that center (vv. 1-2) are in the
past tense, the words on the other side (vv. 4-6) in the future
tense. Present gladness has past and future. It is not an ephemeral emotion. It is not a spurt of good feelings that comes when
the weather and the stock market are both right on the same
day.

The background for joy is only alluded to here, but the words
trigger vast memories: "when GOD returned Israel's exiles. We
laughed, we sang. . . . We were the talk of the nations—'GOD
was wonderful to them!' God *was* wonderful to us; we are one
happy people." What happened that was so "wonderful"? On
nearly any page of the Bible we find the allusions and stories.
There is the story of God's people in a long, apparently intermi-
nable servitude under the shadows of the Egyptian pyramids and
the lash of harsh masters. And then, suddenly and without warn-

ing, it was over. One day they were making "bricks without straw" and the next they were running up the far slopes of the Red Sea, shouting the great song "I'm singing my heart out to GOD—what a victory! He pitched horse and rider into the sea! GOD is my strength. GOD is my song. And, *yes!* GOD is my salvation. *This* is the kind of god I have—I'm telling the world! This is the god of my father—I'm raising the roof!" (Ex 15:1-2).

We turn over a few pages and find the story of David. There were years of wilderness guerrilla warfare against the Philistines, a perilous existence with moody, manic King Saul, and all that painful groping and praying through the guilt of murder and adultery; then in his old age he was chased from his throne by his own son and forced to set up a government in exile. And, at the end, his song. It begins with gratitude: "GOD is bedrock under my feet, the castle in which I live, my rescuing knight"; it ends in confidence, "Live GOD! Blessing from my rock!" In the center there is a rocket burst of joy: "I'm ablaze with your light. . . . I vault the high fences" (2 Sam 22:2, 47, 29-30).

We turn a few more pages and find the terrible story of Babylonian captivity. Israel experienced the worst that can come to any of us: rape in the streets, cannibalism in the kitchens, neighbors reduced to bestiality, a six-hundred-mile forced march across a desert, the taunting mockeries of captors. And then, incredibly—joy. Beginning with the low, gentle words, "Comfort, O comfort my people, says your God. Speak softly and tenderly to Jerusalem, but also firmly and boldly, that she has served her sentence, that her sin is taken care of—forgiven!" (Is 40:1-2). And then the swelling reassurances of help: "When you're in over your head, I'll be there with you. . . . Don't be afraid, I'm with you" (Is 43:2-5). The sounds combine and surge to a proclamation: "How beautiful on the mountains are the feet of the messengers bringing good news. . . . Voices! Listen! Your scouts are shouting, thunderclap shouts, shouting in joyful unison" (52:7-8). The gratitude and gladness build and soar. There is a sea-change into joy.

"It seemed like a dream, too good to be true, when GOD returned Israel's exiles." Each act of God was an impossible miracle. There was no way it could have happened, and it did happen. "It seemed like a dream, too good to be true." We nurture these memories of laughter, these shouts of joy. We fill our minds with the stories of God's acts. Joy has a history. Joy is the verified, repeated experience of those involved in what God is doing. It is as real as a date in history, as solid as a stratum of rock in Palestine. Joy is nurtured by living in such a history, building on such a foundation.

Joyful Expectation

The other side of "we are one happy people"—verses 4-6—is in the future tense. Joy is nurtured by anticipation. If the joy-producing acts of God are characteristic of our past as God's people, they will also be characteristic of our future as his people. There is no reason to suppose that God will arbitrarily change his way of working with us. What we have known of him, we will know of him. Just as joy builds on the past, it borrows from the future. It expects certain things to happen.

Two images fix the hope: The first is "bring rains to our drought-stricken lives." The Negeb, the south of Israel, is a vast desert. The watercourses of the Negeb are a network of ditches cut into the soil by wind and rain erosion. For most of the year they are baked dry under the sun, but a sudden rain makes the desert ablaze with blossoms. Our lives are like that—drought-stricken—and then, suddenly, the long years of barren waiting are interrupted by God's invasion of grace.

The second image is "So those who planted their crops in despair will shout hurrahs at the harvest, / So those who went off with heavy hearts will come home laughing, with armloads of blessing." The hard work of sowing seed in what looks like perfectly empty earth has, as every farmer knows, a time of harvest. All suffering, all pain, all emptiness, all disappointment is seed: sow it in God and he will, finally, bring a crop of joy from it.

It is clear in Psalm 126 that the one who wrote it and those who sang it were no strangers to the dark side of things. They carried the painful memory of exile in their bones and the scars of oppression on their backs. They knew the deserts of the heart and the nights of weeping. They knew what it meant to sow in tears.

One of the most interesting and remarkable things Christians learn is that laughter does not exclude weeping. Christian joy is not an escape from sorrow. Pain and hardship still come, but they are unable to drive out the happiness of the redeemed.

A common but futile strategy for achieving joy is trying to eliminate things that hurt: get rid of pain by numbing the nerve ends, get rid of insecurity by eliminating risks, get rid of disappointment by depersonalizing your relationships. And then try to lighten the boredom of such a life by buying joy in the form of vacations and entertainment. There isn't a hint of that in Psalm 126.

Laughter is a result of living in the midst of God's great works ("when God returned Israel's exiles we laughed, we sang"). Enjoyment is not an escape from boredom but a plunge by faith into God's work ("those who went off with heavy hearts will come home laughing, with armloads of blessing"). There is plenty of suffering on both sides, past and future. The joy comes because God knows how to wipe away tears, and, in his resurrection work, create the smile of new life. Joy is what God gives, not what we work up. Laughter is the delight that things are working together for good to those who love God, not the giggles that betray the nervousness of a precarious defense system. The joy that develops in the Christian way of discipleship is an overflow of spirits that comes from feeling good not about yourself but about God. We find that his ways are dependable, his promises sure.

This joy is not dependent on our good luck in escaping hardship. It is not dependent on our good health and avoidance of pain. Christian joy is actual in the midst of pain, suffering, loneliness and misfortune. St. Paul is our most convincing witness to this. He is always, in one way or another, shouting out his joy. The shouts are tympanic, resonating through every movement of his life: "We continue to shout our praise even when we're hemmed in with troubles, because we know how troubles can develop passionate patience in us, and how that patience in turn forges the tempered steel of virtue, keeping us alert for whatever God will do next. . . . We sing and shout our praises to God through Jesus, the Messiah!" (Rom 5:3-5, 11). That is the fulfillment of the prayer "And now, GOD, do it again—bring rains to our drought-stricken lives."

And then out of his prison cell we hear Paul's trumpeting conclusion to his Philippian letter: "Celebrate God all day, every day. I mean, *revel* in him! Make it as clear as you can to all you meet that you're on their side, working with them and not against them. Help them see that the Master is about to arrive. He could show up any minute!" (Phil 4:4-5). There is no grim Greek Stoicism in that; it is a robust Welsh hymn, striding from sorrow into song. It is the end result of the hope: "So those who went off with heavy hearts will come home laughing, with armloads of blessing." The witness is repeated over and over again, through the generations, and has scattered representatives in every community of Christians.

The psalm does not give us this joy as a package or as a formula, but there are some things it does do. It shows up the tinniness of the world's joy and affirms the solidity of God's joy. It reminds us of the accelerating costs and diminishing returns of those who pursue pleasure as a path toward joy. It introduces us to the way of discipleship, which has consequences in joy. It encourages us in the way of faith to both experience and share joy. It tells the story of God's acts, which put laughter into people's mouths and shouts on their tongues. It repeats the promises of a God who accompanies his wandering, weeping children until they arrive home, exuberant, "with armloads of blessing." It announces the existence of a people who assemble to worship God and disperse to live to God's glory, whose lives are bordered on one side by a memory of God's acts and the other by hope in God's promises, and who along with whatever else is happening are able to say, at the center, "We are one happy people."

9

WORK

"If GOD Doesn't Build the House"

If GOD doesn't build the house,
the builders only build shacks.
If GOD doesn't guard the city,
the night watchman might as well nap.
It's useless to rise early and go to bed late,
and work your worried fingers to the bone.
Don't you know he enjoys
giving rest to those he loves?
Don't you see that children are GOD's best gift?
the fruit of the womb his generous legacy?
Like a warrior's fistful of arrows
are the children of a vigorous youth.
Oh, how blessed are you parents,
with your quivers full of children!
Your enemies don't stand a chance against you;
you'll sweep them right off your doorstep.

PSALM 127

*The first great fact which emerges from our civilization
is that today everything has become "means."
There is no longer an "end"; we do not know whither we are going.
We have forgotten our collective ends, and we possess great means:
we set huge machines in motion in order to arrive nowhere.*

JACQUES ELLUL

The greatest work project of the ancient world is a story of disaster. The unexcelled organization and enormous energy that were concentrated in building the Tower of Babel resulted in such a shattered community and garbled communication that civilization is still trying to recover. Effort, even if the effort is religious (perhaps *especially when* the effort is religious), does not in itself justify anything.

One of the tasks of Christian discipleship is to relearn "the works you did at first" (Rev 2:5 RSV) and absolutely refuse to "work like the devil." Work is a major component in most lives. It is unavoidable. It can be either good or bad, an area where our sin is magnified or where our faith matures. For it is the nature of sin to take good things and twist them, ever so slightly, so that they miss the target to which they were aimed, the target of God. One requirement of discipleship is to learn the ways sin skews our nature and submit what we learn to the continuing will of God, so that we are reshaped through the days of our obedience.

Psalm 127 shows both the right way and the wrong way to work. It posts a warning and provides an example to guide Christians in work that is done to the glory of God.

Babel or Buddhist

Psalm 127 first posts a warning about work: "If GOD doesn't build the house, the builders only build shacks. If GOD doesn't guard the city, the night watchman might as well nap. It's useless to rise early and go to bed late, and work your tired fingers to the bone. Don't you know he enjoys giving rest to those he loves?"

Some people have read these verses and paraphrased them to read like this: "You don't have to work hard to be a Christian. You don't have to put yourself out at all. Go to sleep. God is doing everything that needs to be done." St. Paul had to deal with some of these people in the church at Thessalonica. They were saying that since God had done everything in Christ there was nothing more for them to do. If all effort ends up in godless confusion (as it did with the people at Babel) or in hypocritical self-righteousness (as had happened among the Pharisees), the obvious Christian solution is to quit work and wait for the Lord to come. With a magnificent redeemer like our Lord Jesus Christ and a majestic God like our Father in heaven, what is there left to do? And so they sat around, doing nothing. Meanwhile they lived "by faith" off their less spiritual friends. Unfriendly critics might have called them freeloaders. Paul became angry and told them to get to work: "We're getting reports that a bunch of lazy good-for-nothings are taking advantage of you. This must not be tolerated. We command them to get to work immediately—no excuses, no arguments—and earn their own keep. Friends, don't slack off in doing your duty" (2 Thess 3:11-13). How did they dare to reinterpret the gospel into a rationalization for sloth when he, Paul, from whom they had learned the gospel, worked his fingers "to the bone, up half the night, moonlighting so you wouldn't have the burden of supporting us while we proclaimed God's Message" (1 Thess 2:9).

The Christian has to find a better way to avoid the sin of Babel than by imitating the lilies of the field, which "neither toil nor spin." The pretentious work which became Babel and its pious opposite which developed at Thessalonica are displayed today on the broad canvases of Western and Eastern cultures, respectively.

Western culture takes up where Babel left off and deifies human effort as such. The machine is the symbol of this way of life which attempts to control and manage. Technology promises to give us control over the earth and over other people. But the promise is not fulfilled: lethal automobiles, ugly buildings and ponderous bureaucracies ravage the earth and empty lives of meaning. Structures become more important than the people who live in them. Machines become more important than the people who use them. We care more for our possessions with which we hope to make our way in the world than with our thoughts and dreams which tell us who we are in the world.

Eastern culture, on the other hand, is a variation on the Thessalonian view. It manifests a deep-rooted pessimism regarding human effort. Since all work is tainted with selfishness and pride, the solution is to withdraw from all activity into pure being. The symbol of such an attitude is the Buddha—an enormous fat person sitting cross-legged, looking at his own navel. Motionless, inert, quiet. All trouble comes from doing too much; therefore do nothing. Step out of the rat race. The world of motion is evil, so quit doing everything. Say as little as possible; do as little as possible; finally, at the point of perfection, you will say nothing and do nothing. The goal is to withdraw absolutely and finally from action, from thought, from passion.

The two cultures are in collision today, and many think that we must choose between them. But there is another option: Psalm 127 shows a way to work that is neither sheer activity nor pure passivity. It doesn't glorify work as such, and it doesn't condemn work as such. It doesn't say, "God has a great work for you to do; go and do it." Nor does it say, "God has done everything; go fishing." If we want simple solutions in regard to work, we can become workaholics or dropouts. If we want to experience the fullness of work, we will do better to study Psalm 127.

In the Beginning God Worked

The premise of the psalm for all work is that God works: "If GOD doesn't build the house . . . If GOD doesn't guard the city . . ." The condition *if* presupposes that God does work: he builds; he guards.

The main difference between Christians and others is that we take God seriously and they do not. We really do believe that he is the central reality of all existence. We really do pay attention to what he is and what he does. We really do order our lives in response to that reality and not to some other. Paying attention to God involves a realization that he works.

The Bible begins with the announcement "In the beginning God created"—not "sat majestic in the heavens," not "was filled with beauty and love." He created. He *did* something. He *made* something. He fashioned heaven and earth. The week of creation was a week of work. The days are described not by their weather conditions and not by their horoscope readings: Genesis 1 is a journal of work.

We live in a universe and in a history where God is working. Before anything else, work is an activity of God. Before we go to the sociologists for a description of work or to the psychologists for insight into work or to the economists for an analysis of work, we must comprehend the biblical record: God works. The work of God is defined and described in the pages of Scripture. We have models of creation, acts of redemption, examples of help and compassion, paradigms of comfort and salvation. One of the reasons that Christians read Scripture repeatedly and carefully is to find out just how God works in Jesus Christ so that we can work in the name of Jesus Christ.

In every letter St. Paul wrote, he demonstrated that a Christian's work is a natural, inevitable and faithful development out of God's work. Each of his letters concludes with a series of directives that guide us into the kind of work that participates in God's work. The curse of some people's lives is not work, as such, but senseless work, vain work, futile work, work that takes place apart from God, work that ignores the *if*. Christian discipleship, by orienting us in God's work and setting us in the mainstream of what God is already doing, frees us from the compulsiveness of work. Hilary of Poitiers taught that every Christian must be constantly vigilant against what he called *"irreligiosa solicitudo pro Deo"*—a blasphemous anxiety to do God's work for him.[1]

Our work goes wrong when we lose touch with the God who works "his salvation in the midst of the earth." It goes wrong both when we work anxiously and when we don't work at all, when we become frantic and compulsive in our work (Babel) and when we become indolent and lethargic in our work (Thessalonica). The foundational truth is that work is good. If God does it, it must be all right. Work has dignity: there can be nothing degrading about work if God works. Work has purpose: there can be nothing futile about work if God works.

Effortless Work

The psalm not only posts a warning, it gives an example: "Don't you see that children are GOD's best gift? the fruit of the womb his generous legacy? Like a warrior's fistful of arrows are the children of a vigorous youth. Oh, how blessed are you parents, with your quivers full of children! Your enemies don't stand a chance against you."

In contrast to the anxious labor that builds cities and guards possessions, the psalm praises the effortless work of making children. Opposed to the strenuous efforts of persons who, in doubt of God's providence and mistrust of human love, seek their own gain by godless struggles is the gift of children, born not through human effort but through the miraculous processes of reproduction which God has created among us. The example couldn't have been better chosen. What do we do to get sons and daughters? Very little. The entire miracle of procreation and reproduction requires our participation, but hardly in the form of what we call our work. We did not make these marvelous creatures that walk and talk and grow among us. We participated in an act of love that was provided for us in the structure of God's creation.

Jesus leads us to understand the psalmist's sons in terms representative of all intimate and personal relationships. He himself did not procreate children, yet by his love he made us all sons and daughters (Mt 12:46-50). His job description was "My Father is working straight through. . . . So am I" (Jn 5:17). By joining Jesus and the psalm we learn a way of work that does not acquire things or amass possessions but responds to God and develops relationships. People are at the center of Christian work. In the way of pilgrimage we do not drive cumbersome Conestoga wagons loaded down with baggage over endless prairies. We travel light. The character of our work is shaped not by accomplishments or possessions but in the birth of relationships: "Children are GOD's best gift." We invest our energy in people. Among those around us we develop sons and daughters, sisters and brothers even as our Lord did with us: "Oh, how blessed are you parents with your quivers full of children!"

For it makes very little difference how much money Christians carry in their wallets or purses. It makes little difference

how our culture values and rewards our work . . . *if God doesn't.*
For our work creates neither life nor righteousness. Relentless,
compulsive work habits ("work your worried fingers to the
bone") which our society rewards and admires are seen by the
psalmist as a sign of weak faith and assertive pride, as if God
could not be trusted to accomplish his will, as if we could rear-
range the universe by our own effort.

What does make a difference is the personal relationships
that we create and develop. We learn a name; we start a friendship; we follow up on a smile—or maybe even on a grimace.
Nature is profligate with its seeds, scattering them everywhere;
a few of them sprout. Out of numerous handshakes and greet-
ings, some germinate and grow into a friendship in Christ.
Christian worship gathers the energy and focuses the motivation that transform us from consumers who use work to get
things into people who are intimate and in whom work is a
way of being in creative relationship with another. Such work
can be done within the structure of any job, career or profes-
sion. As Christians do the jobs and tasks assigned to them in
what the world calls work, we learn to pay attention to and
practice what God is doing in love and justice, in helping and
healing, in liberating and cheering.

The first people to sing this psalm had expended much effort
to get to Jerusalem. Some came great distances and overcame
formidable difficulties. Would there be a tendency among the
pilgrims to congratulate one another on their successful journey,
to swell with pride in their accomplishment, to trade stories of
their experiences? Would there be comparisons on who made
the longest pilgrimage, the fastest pilgrimage, who had brought
the most neighbors, who had come the most times? Then,
through the noise of the crowd, someone would strike up the
tune: "If GOD doesn't build . . . guard . . ." The pilgrimage is

not at the center; the Lord is at the center. No matter how hard they had struggled to get there, no matter what they did in the way of heroics—fending off bandits, clubbing lions, crushing wolves—that is not what is to be sung. Psalm 127 insists on a perspective in which our effort is at the periphery and God's work is at the center.

10

HAPPINESS

"Enjoy the Blessing!
Revel in the Goodness!"

All you who fear GOD, how blessed you are!
how happily you walk on his smooth straight road!
You worked hard and deserve all you've got coming.
Enjoy the blessing! Revel in the goodness!
Your wife will bear children as a vine bears grapes,
your household lush as a vineyard,
The children around your table
as fresh and promising as young olive shoots.
Stand in awe of God's Yes.
Oh, how he blesses the one who fears GOD!
Enjoy the good life in Jerusalem
every day of your life.
And enjoy your grandchildren.
Peace to Israel!

PSALM 128

Joy, which was the small publicity of the pagan,
is the gigantic secret of the Christian.

G . K . CHESTERTON

There is a general assumption prevalent in the world that it is extremely difficult to be a Christian. While it is true that many don't completely disqualify themselves as "Christians," they do modify their claims: *ordinary* Christians they call themselves. They respect the church, worship fairly regularly, try to live decently. But they also give themselves somewhat generous margins to allow for the temptations and pressures put upon them by the world. To *really* be on the way of faith, take with absolute *seriousness* all that the Bible says—well, that requires a predisposition to saintliness, extraordinary willpower and an unspecified number of nameless austerities that they are quite sure they cannot manage.

But this is as far from the truth as the east is from the west. The easiest thing in the world is to be a Christian. What is hard is to be a sinner. Being a Christian is what we were created for. The life of faith has the support of an entire creation and the resources of a magnificent redemption. The structure of this world was created by God so we can live in it easily and happily as his children. The history we walk in has been repeatedly entered by God, most notably in Jesus Christ, first to show us and then to help us live full of faith and exuberant with purpose. In the course of Christian discipleship we discover that without Christ we were doing it the hard way and that with Christ we are doing it the easy way. It is not Christians who have it hard, but non-Christians.

Promises and Pronouncements

Blessing is the word that describes this happy state of affairs. Psalm 128 features the word. The psalm begins with three descriptive promises: "All you who fear GOD, how blessed you are!" "You . . . deserve all you've got coming." "Enjoy the blessing! Revel in the goodness!" It concludes with three vigorous pronouncements: "Oh, how he blesses the one who fears GOD!" "Enjoy the good life in Jerusalem." "Enjoy your grandchildren." Sandwiched between those promises and pronouncements is an illustration of blessing: "Your wife will bear children as a vine bears grapes, your household lush as a vineyard, / The children around your table as fresh and promising as young olive shoots."[1]

That all adds up to a good life—a life that is bounded on one side by promises of blessing, on the other side by pronouncements of blessing, and that experiences blessings between those boundaries.

The Bible is one long exposition of this blessing. In Genesis, God, having completed the work of creation by making humankind male and female, "blessed them" (Gen 1:28 RSV). He called Abraham and promised, "I will make of you a great nation, and I will bless you, and make your name great, so that you will be a blessing" (Gen 12:2 RSV). Each of the twelve tribes of Israel receives a special blessing which identifies its particular characteristic of vitality (Gen 49). David, who in so many ways embodied the intensities and joys of faith, was "richer in blessing than any other Israelite"—a long series of blessings, not without sorrow to be sure, but always brimming with life. Jesus, in his introduction to his Sermon on the Mount, identifies the eight key qualities in the life of a person of faith and announces each one with the word *blessed*. He makes it clear that the way of discipleship is not a reduction of what we already are, not an attenuation of our lives, not a subtraction from what we are used to. Rather, he will expand our capacities and fill us up with life so that we overflow with joy. The conclusion of the Bible is that great, thunderous book of Revelation in which there are seven salvos of blessing (1:3; 14:13; 16:15; 19:9; 20:6; 22:7, 14). The blessings cannonade back and forth across the battlefield on which Christ completes his victory over sin and establishes his eternal rule. "The whole book stands in the framework of the blessing of those who attain to and keep the blessed revelation of the mysteries of God (1:3 confirmed in 22:7)."[2]

As we read this story of blessing and familiarize ourselves with the men and women who are experiencing God's blessing, we realize that it is not something external or ephemeral. Not a matter of having a good day, not an occasional run of luck. It is an

> inner strength of the soul—and the happiness it creates, . . . the vital power, without which no living being can exist. Happiness cannot be given to a person as something lying outside him. . . . The action of God does not fall outside but at the very center of the soul; that which it gives us is not something external, but the energy, the power of creating it. . . . The blessing thus comprises the power to live in its deepest and most comprehensive sense. Nothing which belongs to action and to making life real can fall outside the blessing. . . . Blessing is the vital power, without which no living being can exist.[3]

It is this that fills and surrounds the person who is on the way of faith.

Sharing in Life
The illustration that forms the center of the psalm shows how the blessing works: "Your wife will bear children as a vine bears

grapes, your household lush as a vineyard, / The children around your table as fresh and promising as young olive shoots." The illustration is, as we would expect, conditioned by Hebrew culture, in which the standard signs of happiness were a wife who had many children and children who gathered and grew around the table: fruitful vine and olive shoots. This illustration is just that, an example that we need not reproduce exactly in order to experience blessing. (We, for instance, don't try to have as many children as possible—or try to get them to stay at home for all their lives!) But the meaning is still with us: Blessing has inherent in it the power to increase. It functions by sharing and delight in life. "Life consists in the constant meeting of souls, which must share their contents with each other. The blessed gives to the others, because the strength instinctively pours from him and up around him. . . . The characteristic of blessing is to multiply."[4]

John Calvin, preaching to his congregation in Geneva, Switzerland, pointed out that we must develop better and deeper concepts of happiness than those held by the world, which makes a happy life to consist in "ease, honours, and great wealth."[5] Psalm 128 helps us do that. Too much of the world's happiness depends on taking from one to satisfy another. To increase my standard of living, people in another part of the world must lower theirs. The worldwide crisis of hunger that we face today is a result of that method of pursuing happiness. Industrialized nations acquire appetites for more and more luxuries and higher and higher standards of living, and increasing numbers of people are made poor and hungry. It doesn't have to be that way. The experts on the world hunger problem say that there is enough to go around right now. We don't have a production problem. We have the agricultural capability to produce enough food. We have the transportation technology to distribute the food. But we have a greed problem: if I don't grab mine while I can, I might not be happy. The hunger problem is not going to be solved by government or by industry but in church, among Christians who learn a different way to pursue happiness.

Christian blessing is a realizing that "it is more blessed to give than to receive." As we learn to give and to share, our vitality increases, and the people around us become fruitful vines and olive shoots at our tables.

The blessings that are promised to, pronounced upon and experienced by Christians do not of course exclude difficulties. The Bible never indicates that. But the difficulties are not inherent in the faith: they come from the outside in the form of temptations, seductions, pressures. Not a day goes by but what we have to deal with that ancient triple threat that Christians in the Middle Ages summarized under the headings of the world, the flesh and the devil: the world—the society of proud and arrogant humankind that defies and tries to eliminate God's rule and presence in history; the flesh—the corruption that sin has introduced into our very appetites and instincts; and the devil— the malignant will that tempts and seduces us away from the will of God. We have to contend with all of that. We are in a battle. There is a fight of faith to be waged.

But the way of faith itself is in tune with what God has done and is doing. The road we travel is the well-traveled road of discipleship. It is not a way of boredom or despair or confusion. It is not a miserable groping but a way of blessing.

Traveling by the Roads

There are no tricks involved in getting in on this life of blessing, and no luck required. We simply become Christians and begin the life of faith. We acknowledge God as our maker and lover and accept Christ as the means by which we can be in living relationship with God. We accept the announced and proclaimed truth that God is at the center of our existence, find out how he has constructed this world (his creation), how he has provided for our redemption, and proceed to walk in that way. In the plain words of the psalm: "All you who fear GOD, how blessed you are! how happily you walk on his smooth straight road!"

"Fear GOD." *Reverence* might be a better word. *Awe.* The Bible isn't interested in whether we believe in God or not. It assumes that everyone more or less does. What it is interested in is the response we have to him: Will we let God be as he is, majestic and holy, vast and wondrous, or will we always be trying to whittle him down to the size of our small minds, insist on confining him within the boundaries we are comfortable with, refuse to think of him other than in images that are convenient to our lifestyle? But then we are not dealing with the God of creation and the Christ of the cross, but with a dime-store reproduction of something made in our image, usually for commercial reasons. To guard against all such blasphemous chumminess with the Almighty, the Bible talks of the fear of the Lord—not to scare us but to bring us to awesome attention before the overwhelming grandeur of God, to shut up our whining and chattering and stop our running and fidgeting so that we can really see him as he is and listen to him as he speaks his merciful, life-changing words of forgiveness.

"Walk on his smooth straight road." Not only do we let God be God as he really is, but we start doing the things for which he made us. We take a certain route; we follow certain directions; we do specified things. There are ethical standards to follow, there are moral values to foster, there are spiritual disciplines to practice, there is social justice to pursue, there are personal relationships to develop. None of it is difficult to understand. "Mere ethics," quipped Austin Farrer once, "call for no such august or mysterious explanation; next to plumbing, morality is social convenience number one."[6]

Because of the ambiguities of the world we live in and the defects in our own wills, we will not do any of this perfectly and without fault. But that isn't the point. The way is plain—walk in it. Keeping the rules and obeying the commands is only common sense. People who are forever breaking the rules, trying other roads, attempting to create their own system of values and truth from scratch, spend most of their time calling up someone to get them out of trouble and help repair the damage, and then ask the silly question "What went wrong?" As H. H. Farmer said, "If you go against the grain of the universe you get splinters."

Some who read Psalm 128 will say, "Of course, that's the way it is with me. Doesn't everyone feel that?" Others will only be puzzled by how anyone could sing such a cheerful song in such a messed-up world. John Henry Newman once explained it this way: "If I want to travel north and all the roads are cut to the east, of course I shall complain of the roads. I shall find nothing but obstacles; I shall have to surmount walls, and cross rivers, and go round about, and after all fail of my end." Such is the conduct of those who are trying to achieve some meaning in their lives, pursuing their right to happiness, but refusing to take the well-traveled roads that lead there. They are trying to get to Mount Zion but ignore all the signposts and compass readings and stubbornly avoid the trails as they bushwhack their way through wilderness. "Do you not see that they necessarily must meet with thwartings, crossings, disappointments, and failure?" They go mile after mile, watching for their destination but never sighting it. "And then they accuse religion of interfering with what they consider their innocent pleasures and wishes." But religion is an inconvenience only to those who are traveling against the grain of creation, at cross-purposes with the way that leads to redemption.[7]

Everyone wants to be happy, to be blessed. Too many people are willfully refusing to pay attention to the One who wills our happiness and ignorantly supposing that the Christian way is a harder way to get what they want than doing it on their own. They are wrong. God's ways and God's presence are where we experience the happiness that lasts. Do it the easy way: "All you who fear GOD, how blessed you are! how happily you walk on his smooth straight road!"

11

PERSEVERANCE

"They Never Could Keep Me Down"

"They've kicked me around ever since I was young"
—this is how Israel tells it—
"They've kicked me around ever since I was young,
but they never could keep me down.
Their plowmen plowed long furrows
up and down my back;
But GOD wouldn't put up with it,
he sticks with us;
Then GOD ripped the harnesses
of the evil plowmen to shreds."
Oh, let all those who hate Zion
grovel in humiliation;
Let them be like grass in shallow ground
that withers before the harvest,
Before the farmhands can gather it in,
the harvesters get in the crop,
Before the neighbors have a chance to call out,
"Congratulations on your wonderful crop!
We bless you in GOD's name!"

PSALM 129

Patience is drawing on underlying forces; it is powerfully positive,
though to a natural view it looks like just sitting it out.
How would I persist against positive eroding forces if
I were not drawing on invisible forces?
And patience has a positive tonic effect on others;
because of the presence of the patient person,
they revive and go on, as if he were the gyroscope of the ship providing
a stable ground. But the patient person himself does not enjoy it.

PAUL GOODMAN

S tick-to-itiveness is one of the more inelegant words in the English language, but I have a special fondness for it. I heard the word a great deal when I was young, mostly, as I recall, from my mother. I was a creature of sudden but short-lived enthusiasms. I had a passion for building model airplanes, and then one day, mysteriously, all desire left and the basement was left littered with half-finished models. Then stamp collecting became an all-consuming hobby. I received an immense stamp album for Christmas, joined a philatelic club, acquired piles and piles of stamps, and then one day, unaccountably, the interest left me. The album gathered dust and the mounds of stamps were left unmounted. Next it was horses. Each Saturday morning my best friend and I would ride our bikes to a dude ranch two miles from town, get horses and ride up into the Montana foothills imagining we were Merriwether Lewis and William Clark or, less pretentiously, Gene Autry and the Lone Ranger. And then, overnight, that entire world vanished and in its place was—girls.

It was during these rather frequent transitions from one enthusiasm to another that I was slapped with the reprimand "Eugene, you have no stick-to-itiveness. You never finish anything." Years later I learned that the church had a fancier word for the same thing: *perseverance*. I have also found that it is one of the marks of Christian discipleship and have learned to admire those who exemplify it. Along the way Psalm 129 has gotten included in my admiration.

Tough Faith

" 'They've kicked me around ever since I was young'—this is how Israel tells it—'They've kicked me around ever since I was young, but they never could keep me down.' " The people of God are tough. For long centuries those who belong to the world have waged war against the way of faith, and they have yet to win. They have tried everything, but none of it has worked. They have tried persecution and ridicule, torture and exile, but the way of faith has continued healthy and robust: "They've kicked me around ever since I was young, but they never could keep me down."

Do you think of Christian faith as a fragile style of life that can flourish only when weather conditions are just right, or do you see it as a tough perennial that can stick it out through storm and drought, survive the trampling of careless feet and the attacks of vandals? Here is a biblical writer's view: "He grew up before God, a scrawny seedling, a scrubby plant in a parched field. . . . He was looked down on and passed over, a man who suffered, knew pain firsthand. . . . One look at him and people turned away" (Is 53:1-3). It is a portrait of extreme rejection and painful persecution. What could come of such a poor, precarious beginning? Not much, it would seem. Yet look at the results: "He'll see life come from it, life, life and more life, and God's plan will prosper through what he does. Out of that terrible travail of soul, he'll see that it's worth it and be glad he did it. Through what he learned, my righteous one, my servant, will make many 'righteous ones,' carrying himself the burden of their sins" (Is 53:10-11). The person of faith outlasts all the oppressors. Faith lasts.

We remember the way it was with Jesus. His ministry began with forty days of temptation in the desert and concluded in that never-to-be-forgotten night of testing and trial in Gethsemane and Jerusalem. Has anyone ever experienced such a relentless, merciless pounding from within and from without? First there were the cunning attempts to get him off the track, every temptation disguised as a suggestion for improvement, offered with the best of intentions to help Jesus in the ministry on which he had so naively and innocently set out. Then, at the other end, when all the temptations had failed, that brutal assault when his body was turned into a torture chamber. And we know the result: an incomprehensible kindness ("Father, forgive them"), an unprecedented serenity ("Father, into your hands I commit my spirit") and—resurrection.

And Paul. His life recklessly caromed from adversity to persecution and back to adversity. In one passage he looks back and summarizes:

> I have been beaten times without number. I have faced death again and again. I have been beaten the regulation thirty-nine stripes by the Jews five times. I have been beaten with rods three times. I have been stoned once. I have been shipwrecked three times. I have been twenty-four hours in the open sea. In my travels I have been in constant danger from rivers, from bandits, from my own countrymen, and from pagans. I have faced danger in city streets, danger in the desert, danger on the high seas, danger among false Christians. I have known drudgery, exhaustion, many sleepless nights, hunger and thirst, fasting, cold and exposure. Apart from all external trials I have the daily burden of responsibility for all the churches. Do you think anyone is weak without my feeling his weakness? Does anyone have his faith upset without my burning with indignation? (2 Cor 11:23-29 Phillips)

None of that had the power to push Paul off his path. None of it convinced him that he was on the wrong way. None of it persuaded him that he had made the wrong choice years earlier

on the Damascus Road. At the end of his life, among the last
words he wrote is this sentence: "I've got my eye on the goal,
where God is beckoning us onward—to Jesus. I'm off and running, and I'm not turning back" (Phil 3:13-14).

Stick-to-itiveness. Perseverance. Patience. The way of faith is not
a fad that is taken up in one century only to be discarded in the
next. It lasts. It is a way that works. It has been tested thoroughly.

Cut Cords, Withered Grass

An interesting line in Psalm 129 provides a detail that is both
fascinating and useful. The sentence is "Then GOD ripped the
harnesses of the evil plowmen to shreds." The previous verse
provides the context: "Their plowmen plowed long furrows up
and down my back." Picture Israel, the person of faith, lying
stretched out, prone. The enemies hitch up their oxen and
plows and begin cutting long furrows in the back of Israel. Long
gashes cut into the skin and flesh, back and forth, systematically,
like a farmer working a field. Imagine the whole thing: the
blood, the pain, the back-and-forth cruelty.

And then, suddenly, the realization that there was no more
hurting. The oxen were still tramping back and forth, the oxherds were still shouting their commands, but the plows were
not working. "GOD ripped the harnesses of the evil plowmen to
shreds." The harness cords, connecting plow to oxen, have been
severed. The plows of persecution aren't working, and the oxherds haven't even noticed! They plod back and forth, unaware
that their opposition is worthless. They are wasting their time
and energy. The wicked oxherds are comic figures, solemnly and
efficiently doing their impressive work, proudly puffed with self-
importance, thinking of what they are accomplishing historically
on the back of Israel. If they ever looked behind them (which
they never do—their stiff necks make that exercise too painful),

they would see that their bluster and blasphemy are having no results at all: "GOD ripped the harnesses of the evil plowmen to shreds."

The concluding illustration in the psalm tells a similar truth. Opposition to the people of faith is like "grass in shallow ground." Palestine is a rocky country; in many places there is only a thin layer of soil over bedrock. Seeds would sprout and grow from this dirt, but the grass didn't last; the thin soil couldn't support it. By midday the grass would wither. No harvest there. No reapers wasting their time there. No one going along the road would ever look and shout out, "Great harvest you have there. God's blessing upon you!" The illustration is a cartoon, designed to bring a smile to the people of faith.

The life of the world that is opposed or indifferent to God is barren and futile. It is plowing a field, thinking you are tramping all over God's people and cutting his purposes to ribbons, but unaware that long ago your plow was disengaged. It is naively thinking you might get a harvest of grain from that shallow patch of dirt on a shelf of rock. The way of the world is peppered with brief enthusiasms, like the grass on that half-inch of topsoil, springing up so wonderfully and without effort, but as quickly withering. The way of the world is marked by proud, God-defying purposes, unharnessed from eternity and therefore worthless and futile.

The Passion of Patience
There is one phrase in this psalm that good taste would prefer to delete but that honesty must deal with: "Oh, let all who hate Zion grovel in humiliation." Anger seethes and pulses in the wounds. A sense of wrong has been festering. Accumulated resentment wants vindication.

However much we feel the inappropriateness of this kind of

thing in a man or woman of faith, we must also admit to its authenticity. For who does not experience flashes of anger at those who make our way hard and difficult? There are times in the long obedience of Christian discipleship when we get tired and fatigue draws our tempers short. At such times to see someone flitting from one sensation, one enthusiasm, to another, quitting on commitments, ducking responsibilities, provokes our anger—and sometimes piques our envy. No matter that we are, on other grounds, convinced that their adulteries are an admission of boredom, that their pleasures are the shallowest of distractions from which they must return to worsening anxieties and an emptier loneliness. Even when we know we are doing good work that has a good future, the foolery and enmity of these others make a hard day harder, and anger flares.

We can't excuse the psalmist for getting angry on the grounds that he was not yet a Christian, for he had Leviticus to read: "You shall not hate your brother in your heart. . . . You shall not take vengeance or bear any grudge against the sons of your own people, but you shall love your neighbor as yourself" (Lev 19:17-18 RSV). And he had Exodus: "If you meet your enemy's ox or his ass going astray, you shall bring it back to him. If you see the ass of one who hates you lying under its burden, you shall refrain from leaving him with it; you shall help him to lift it up" (Ex 23:4-5 RSV). And he had Proverbs: "Don't laugh when your enemy falls; don't crow over his collapse" (Prov 24:17). When Jesus said "Love your enemies," he added nothing to what this psalmist already had before him.

So we will not make excuses for the psalmist's vindictiveness. What we will do is admire its energy. For it is apathetic, sluggish neutrality that is death to perseverance, acts like a virus in the bloodstream and enervates the muscles of discipleship. The person who makes excuses for hypocrites and rationalizes the excesses of the wicked, who loses a sense of opposition to sin, who obscures the difference between faith and denial, grace and self-ishness—*that* is the person to be wary of. For if there is not all that much difference between the way of faith and the ways of the world, there is not much use in making any effort to stick to it.

We drift on the tides of convenience. We float on fashions. It is regarding the things we care about that we are capable of expressing anger. A parent sees a child dart out into a roadway and narrowly miss being hit by a car, and angrily yells at the child, at the driver—at both. The anger may not be the most appropriate expression of concern, but it is evidence of concern. Indifference would be inhuman.

And so here. The psalms are not sung by perfect pilgrims. The pilgrims of old made their mistakes, just as we make ours. *Perseverance* does not mean "perfection." It means that we keep going. We do not quit when we find that we are not yet mature and there is a long journey still before us. We get caught yelling at our wives, at our husbands, at our friends, at our employers, at our employees, at our children. Our yelling (though not all of it!) means we care about something: we care about God; we care about the ways of the kingdom; we care about morality, about justice, about righteousness. The way of faith centers and absorbs our lives, and when someone makes the way difficult, throws stumbling blocks in the path of the innocent, creates difficulties for those young in faith and unpracticed in obedience, there is anger: "Oh, let all those who hate Zion grovel in humiliation!"

For perseverance is not resignation, putting up with things the way they are, staying in the same old rut year after year after year, or being a doormat for people to wipe their feet on. Endurance is not a desperate hanging on but a traveling from strength to strength. There is nothing fatigued or humdrum in Isaiah, nothing flatfooted in Jesus, nothing jejune in Paul. Perseverance is triumphant and alive.

The psalmist lived among prophets and priests who dealt with his vindictive spirit and nurtured him toward a better way of treating the wicked than calling down curses on them, learning what Charles Williams once described as the "passion of patience." We are in a similar apprenticeship. But we will not learn it by swallowing our sense of outrage on the one hand or, on the other, excusing all wickedness as a neurosis. We will do it by offering up our anger to God, who trains us in creative love.

God Sticks with Us

The cornerstone sentence of Psalm 129 is "GOD wouldn't put up with it, he sticks with us." When the Bible says that God sticks with us, the emphasis is on his dependable personal relationship, that he is always *there* for us. The phrase does not mean that he corresponds to some abstract ideal of what is right; it speaks of a personal right relationship between Creator and creation. "Righteous" is a common translation for the Hebrew term. "Righteous is out and out a term denoting relationship, and . . . it does this in the sense of referring to a real relationship between two parties . . . and not to the relationship of an object under consideration to an idea."[1]

That "he sticks with us" is the reason Christians can look back over a long life crisscrossed with cruelties, unannounced tragedies, unexpected setbacks, sufferings, disappointments, depressions—look back across all that and see it as a road of blessing, and make a song out of what we see. "They've kicked me around ever since I was young, but they never could keep me down." God sticks to his relationship. He establishes a personal relationship with us and stays with it. The central reality for Christians is the personal, unalterable, persevering commitment God makes to us. Perseverance is not the result of *our* determination, it is the result of God's faithfulness. We survive in the way of faith not because we have extraordinary stamina but because God is righteous, because God sticks with us. Christian discipleship is a process of paying more and more attention to God's righteousness and less and less attention to our own; finding the meaning of our lives not by probing our moods and motives and morals but by believing in God's will and purposes; making a map of the faithfulness of God, not charting the rise and fall of our enthusiasms. It is out of such a reality that we acquire perseverance.

This is what the writer of the New Testament letter to the Hebrew Christians did. He sang a litany of people who lived by faith, that is, people who centered their lives on the righteous God who stuck by them through thick and thin so that they were able to persevere. They lived with uncommon steadiness of purpose and with a most admirable integrity. None of them lived without sin. They all made their share of mistakes and engaged in episodes of disobedience and rebellion. But God stuck with them so consistently and surely that they learned how to stick with God. Out of that litany comes this call:

> Strip down, start running—and never quit! No extra spiritual fat, no parasitic sins. Keep your eyes on *Jesus,* who both began and finished this race we're in. Study how he did it. Because he never lost sight of where he was headed—that exhilarating finish in and with God—he could put up with anything along the way: cross, shame, whatever. And now he's *there,* in the place of honor, right alongside God. (Heb 12:1-2)

Some of those early Christians this writer was addressing had been complaining, apparently, that life was too rough for them. They couldn't hold out any longer (complaints that are, from time to time, heard in every congregation). They didn't see the use in believing in a God they never saw, serving a God who didn't give them what they want, trusting a God who let babies die and good people suffer. There is a no-nonsense slap of reality in the words their pastor addressed to them: "In this all-out match against sin, others have suffered far worse than you, to say nothing of what Jesus went through—all that bloodshed!" (Heb 12:3). Quit your complaining. Take a look at the pilgrim road and see where you have come from and where you are going. Take up the refrains of the great song. " 'They've kicked me around ever since I was young'—this is how Israel tells it—'They've kicked me around ever since I was young, but they never could keep me down.' "

Purposes Last
The reason my childhood was one enthusiasm after another was that I hadn't yet found an organizing center for my life and a goal that would demand my all and my best. The Christian faith is the discovery of that center in the God who sticks with us, the righteous God. Christian discipleship is a decision to walk in his ways, steadily and firmly, and then finding that the way integrates all our interests, passions and gifts, our human needs and our eternal aspirations. It is the way of life we were created for. There are endless challenges in it to keep us on the growing edge of faith; there is always the God who sticks with us to make it possible for us to persevere.

In Charles Williams's delightful, brief drama *Grab and Grace,* there is a dialogue between Grace and a man who is dabbling in religion, trying out different experiences, "into yoga one week, buddhism the next, spiritualism the next." Grace mentions the Holy Spirit. Grab says, "The Holy Spirit? Good. We will ask him to come while I am in the mood, which passes so quickly and then all is so dull."

And Grace answers: "Sir, purposes last."

12

HOPE

"I Pray to GOD . . . and Wait for What He'll Say & Do"

Help, GOD—the bottom has fallen out of my life!
Master, hear my cry for help!
Listen hard! Open your ears!
Listen to my cries for mercy.
If you, GOD, kept records on wrongdoings,
who would stand a chance?
As it turns out, forgiveness is your habit,
and that's why you're worshiped.
I pray to GOD—my life a prayer—
and wait for what he'll say and do.
My life's on the line before God, my Lord,
waiting and watching till morning,
waiting and watching till morning.
Oh Israel, wait and watch for GOD—
with GOD's arrival comes love,
with GOD's arrival comes generous redemption.
No doubt about it—he'll redeem Israel,
buy back Israel from captivity to sin.

PSALM 130

*Hope is a projection of the imagination; so is despair. Despair all
too readily embraces the ills it foresees; hope is an energy and
arouses the mind to explore every possibility to combat them. . . .
In response to hope the imagination is aroused to picture every
possible issue, to try every door, to fit together even the most heterogeneous
pieces in the puzzle. After the solution has been found it is difficult
to recall the steps taken—so many of them are just below
the level of consciousness.*

THORNTON WILDER

To be human is to be in trouble. Job's anguish is our epigraph: "Man is born to trouble as the sparks fly upward." Suffering is a characteristic of the personal. Animals can be hurt, but they do not suffer. The earth can be ravaged, yet it cannot suffer. Man and woman, alone in the creation, suffer. For suffering is pain *plus:* physical or emotional pain *plus* the awareness that our own worth as people is threatened, that our own value as creatures made in the dignity of God is called into question, that our own destiny as eternal souls is jeopardized. Are we to be, finally, nothing? Are we to be discarded? Are we to be rejects in the universe and thrown onto the garbage dump of humanity because our bodies degenerate or our emotions malfunction or our minds become confused or our families find fault with us or society avoids us? Any one of these things, or, as is more likely, a combination of them, can put us in the state Psalm 130 describes as "the bottom has fallen out of my life!"

A Christian is a person who decides to face and live through suffering. If we do not make that decision, we are endangered on every side. A man or woman of faith who fails to acknowledge and deal with suffering becomes, at last, either a cynic or a melancholic or a suicide. Psalm 130 grapples mightily with suffering, sings its way through it, and provides usable experience for those who are committed to traveling the way of faith to God through Jesus Christ.

Giving Dignity to Suffering

The psalm begins in pain: "Help, GOD—the botton has fallen out of my life! Master, hear my cry for help! Listen hard! Open your ears! Listen to my cries for mercy." The psalm is anguished prayer.

By setting the anguish out in the open and voicing it as a prayer, the psalm gives dignity to our suffering. It does not look on suffering as something slightly embarrassing that must be hushed up and locked in a closet (where it finally becomes a skeleton) because this sort of thing shouldn't happen to a real person of faith. And it doesn't treat it as a puzzle that must be explained, and therefore turn it over to theologians or philosophers to work out an answer. Suffering is set squarely, openly, passionately before God. It is acknowledged and expressed. It is described and lived.

If the psalm did nothing more than that, it would be a prize, for it is difficult to find anyone in our culture who will respect us when we suffer. We live in a time when everyone's goal is to be perpetually healthy and constantly happy. If any one of us fails to live up to the standards that are advertised as normative, we are labeled as a problem to be solved, and a host of well-intentioned people rush to try out various cures on us. Or we are looked on as an enigma to be unraveled, in which case we are subjected to endless discussions, our lives examined by researchers zealous for the clue that will account for our lack of health or happiness. Ivan Illich, in an interview, said: "You know, there is an American myth that denies suffering and the sense of pain. It acts as if they *should* not be, and hence it devalues the *experience* of suffering. But this myth denies our encounter with reality."[1]

The gospel offers a different view of suffering: in suffering we enter *the depths;* we are at the heart of things; we are near to where Christ was on the cross. P. T. Forsyth wrote:

The depth is simply the height inverted, as sin is the index of moral grandeur. The cry is not only truly human, but divine as well. God is deeper than the deepest depth in man. He is holier than our deepest sin is deep. There is no depth so deep to us as when God reveals his holiness in dealing with our sin. . . . [And so] think more of the depth of God than the depth of your cry. The worst thing that can happen to a man is to have no God to cry to out of the depth.[2]

Israel teaches us to respond to suffering as reality, not deny it as illusion, and leads us to face it with faith, not avoid it out of terror. The psalm in this way is representative of Israel, which

took a supremely realistic view of life's sufferings and dangers, saw herself as exposed to them vulnerably and without defence, and showed little talent for fleeing from them into ideologies of any kind. Rather, concepts of her faith directed her to bring these actual experiences of her daily life into connexion with Jahweh. In her older period, indeed, she lacked any aptitude for the doctrinaire: she possessed, rather, an exceptional strength to face up even to negative realities, to recognize and not to repress them, even when she was spiritually unable to master them in any way. It is to this realism, which allowed every event its own inevitability and validity, . . . that the narrative art of the OT, especially in its earlier form, owes its darksome grandeur.[3]

And so we find in Psalm 130 not so much as a trace of those things that are so common among us, which rob us of our humanity when we suffer and make the pain so much more terrible to bear. No glib smart answers. No lectures on our misfortunes in which we are hauled into a classroom and given graduate courses in suffering. No hasty Band-Aid treatments covering up our trouble so that the rest of society does not have to look at it. Neither prophets nor priests nor psalmists offer quick cures for the suffering: we don't find any of them telling us to take a vacation, use this drug, get a hobby. Nor do they ever engage in publicity cover-ups, the plastic-smile propaganda campaigns that hide trouble behind a billboard of positive thinking. None of that: the suffering is held up and proclaimed—and prayed.

Not that Christians celebrate suffering—we don't make a religion out of it. We are not masochists who think we are being holy when we are hurting, who think personal misery is a sign of exceptional righteousness. There is some suffering in which we get involved that is useless and unnecessary; but there is adequate commonsense wisdom in Christian ways which prevents us from suffering for the wrong reasons, if only we will pay attention to it. Henri Nouwen wrote:

> Many people suffer because of the false supposition on which they have based their lives. That supposition is that there should be no fear or loneliness, no confusion or doubt. But these sufferings can only be dealt with creatively when they are understood as wounds integral to our human condition. Therefore ministry is a very *confronting* service. It does not allow people to live with illusions of immortality and wholeness. It keeps reminding others that they are mortal and broken, but also that with the recognition of this condition, liberation starts.[4]

George MacDonald put it with epigrammatic force: "The Son of God suffered unto the death, not that men might not suffer, but that their sufferings might be like His."[5]

The second important thing Psalm 130 does is to immerse the suffering in God—all the suffering is spoken in the form of prayer, which means that God is taken seriously as a personal and concerned being. Certain sentences in the psalm show specific knowledge of the character of God as a personal redeemer: God is personal so that we may have an intimate relation with him; God is redeemer so that we may be helped by him. There is *meaning to* our lives and there is *salvation for* our lives, a truth summed up by Forsyth when he said, "Our very pain is a sign of God's remembrance of us, for it would be much worse if we were left in ghastly isolation."[8]

Eight times the name of God is used in the psalm. We find, as we observe how God is addressed, that he is understood as One who forgives sin, who comes to those who wait and hope for him, who is characterized by steadfast love and plenteous redemption, and who will redeem Israel. God makes a difference. God acts positively toward his people. God is not indifferent. He is not rejecting. He is not ambivalent or dilatory. He does not act arbitrarily, in fits and starts. He is not stingy, providing only for bare survival. Karl Barth describes God in this regard:

> The free inclination of God to His creature, denoted in the Biblical witness by grace, takes place under the presupposition that the creature is in distress and that God's intention is to espouse his cause and to grant him assistance in his extremity. Because grace, the gracious love of God, consists in this inclination, it is, and therefore God Himself is, merciful; God's very being is mercy. The mercy of God lies in His readiness to share in sympathy the distress of another, a readiness which springs from His inmost nature and stamps all His being and doing. It lies, therefore, in His will, springing from the depths of His nature and characterising it, to take the initiative Himself for the removal of this distress. For the fact that God participates in it by sympathy implies that He is really present in its midst, and this means again that He wills that it should not be, that He wills therefore to remove it.[7]

And this, of course, is why we are able to face, acknowledge, accept and live through suffering: we know that it can never be ultimate, it can never constitute the bottom line. God is at the foundation and God is at the boundaries. God seeks the hurt, maimed, wandering and lost. God woos the rebellious and con-

fused. If God were different than he is, not one of us would
have a leg to stand on: "If you, GOD, kept records on wrongdoings, who would stand a chance? As it turns out, forgiveness is
your habit, and that's why you're worshiped." Because of the
forgiveness we have a place to stand. We stand in confident awe
before God, not in terrorized despair.

Employed to Wait
Such are the two great realities of Psalm 130: suffering is real;
God is real. Suffering is a mark of our existential authenticity;
God is proof of our essential and eternal humanity. We accept
suffering; we believe in God. The acceptance and the belief both
emerge out of those times when "the bottom has fallen out" of
our lives.

But there is more than a description of reality here, there is a
procedure for participating in it. The program is given in two
words: *wait* and *watch*. The words are at the center of the psalm.
"I pray to GOD—my life a prayer—and wait for what he'll say
and do. My life's on the line before God, my Lord, waiting and
watching till morning, waiting and watching till morning." *Wait*
and *watch* add up to *hope*.

The words *wait* and *hope* are connected with the image of
watchmen waiting through the night for the dawn. The connection provides important insights for the person in trouble who
cries out, "But surely there is something for me to do!" The answer is yes, there is something for you to do, or more exactly
there is someone you can *be:* be a watchman.

A watchman is an important person, but he doesn't do very
much. The massive turning of the earth, the immense energies
released by the sun—all that goes on apart from him. He does
nothing to influence or control such things: he is a watchman.
He knows the dawn is coming; there are no doubts concerning

that. Meanwhile he is alert to dangers; he comforts restless children or animals until it is time to work or play again in the light of day.

I was once a watchman. I worked from 10 p.m. until 6 a.m. in a building in New York City. My work as a night watchman was combined with that of elevator operator, but the elevator work petered out about midnight. After that I sat and read, dozed or studied. There were assorted night people in the neighborhood who would stop in through the night hours and visit with me: strange, bizarre people with wonderful stories. I will never know how much of what I heard from them was fact and how much fiction: a failed millionaire obsessed with communist plots responsible for his decline, a South American adventurer now too old to tramp the remote jungles and mountains, a couple of streetwalkers who on slow nights would sit and talk about God and the worth of their souls.

I did that for an entire year. I stayed awake, I studied, I learned. I visited and gossiped. And I waited for the dawn. Dawn always came. The people who employed me thought it was worth several dollars an hour for me to wait through the night and watch for the morning. But I never did anything, never constructed anything, never made anything happen. I waited and watched. I hoped.

If I had not known that there were others in charge of the building, I might not have been content to just be a watchman and collect my pay. If I were not confident that the building had an owner who cared about it, if I did not know that there was a building engineer who kept it in good order and repair, if I did not know that there were hundreds of people in the building who were going about their work everyday quite capably—if I had not known these things, I might not have been so relaxed in making idle gossip with women of the night and old men of storied pasts. Nor would the psalmist have been content to be a watchman if he were not sure of God. The psalmist's and the Christian's waiting and watching—that is, hoping—is based on the conviction that God is actively involved in his creation and vigorously at work in redemption.

Hoping does not mean doing nothing. It is not fatalistic resignation. It means going about our assigned tasks, confident that God will provide the meaning and the conclusions. It is not compelled to work away at keeping up appearances with a bogus spirituality. It is the opposite of desperate and panicky manipulations, of scurrying and worrying.

And hoping is not dreaming. It is not spinning an illusion or fantasy to protect us from our boredom or our pain. It means a confident, alert expectation that God will do what he said he will do. It is imagination put in the harness of faith. It is a willingness to let God do it his way and in his time. It is the opposite of making plans that we demand that God put into effect, telling him both how and when to do it. That is not hoping in God but bullying God. "I pray to GOD—my life a prayer—and wait for what he'll say and do. My life's on the line before God, my Lord, waiting and watching till morning, waiting and watching till morning."

An Eye Specialist and a Painter

When we suffer we attract counselors as money attracts thieves. Everybody has an idea of what we did wrong to get ourselves into such trouble and a prescription for what we can do to get out of it. We are flooded first with sympathy and then with advice, and when we don't come around quickly we are abandoned as a hopeless case. But none of that is what we need. We need hope. We need to know that we are in relation to God. We need to know that suffering is part of what it means to be human and not something alien. We need to know where *we* are and where *God* is.

We need an eye specialist rather, than, say, a painter. A painter tries to convey to us with the aid of his brush and palette a picture of the world as he sees it; an ophthalmologist tries to enable us to see the world as it really is. In George MacDonald's novel *The Princess and Curdie*, when Curdie reaches the castle, he sees the great staircase and knows that to reach the tower he must go farther. The narrator takes the occasion to note that "those who work well in the depths more easily understand the heights, for indeed in their true nature they are one and the same."[8]

For the person who suffers, has suffered or will suffer, Psalm 130 is essential equipment, for it convinces us that the big difference is not in what people suffer but in the way they suffer. ("The same shaking that makes fetid water stink makes perfume issue a more pleasant odor.")[9] The psalm does not exhort us to put up with suffering; it does not explain it or explain it away. It is, rather, a powerful demonstration that our place in the depths is not out of bounds from God. We see that whatever or whoever got us in trouble cannot separate us from God, for "forgiveness is your habit." We are persuaded that God's way with us is redemption and that the redemption, not the suffering, is ultimate.

The "bottom" has a bottom; the heights are boundless. Knowing that, we are helped to go ahead and learn the skills of waiting and watching—hoping!—by which God is given room to work out our salvation and develop our faith while we fix our attention on his ways of grace and resurrection.

13

HUMILITY

"I've Kept My Feet on the Ground"

GOD, I'm not trying to rule the roost,
I don't want to be king of the mountain.
I haven't meddled where I have no business
or fantasized grandiose plans.
I've kept my feet on the ground,
I've cultivated a quiet heart.
Like a baby content in its mother's arms,
my soul is a baby content.
Wait, Israel, for GOD. Wait with hope.
Hope now; hope always!

PSALM 131

Humility is the obverse side of confidence in God,
whereas pride is the obverse side of confidence in self.

JOHN BAILLIE

Christian faith needs continuous maintenance. It requires attending to. "If you leave a thing alone you leave it to a torrent of change. If you leave a white post alone it will soon be a black post."[1]

Every spring in my neighborhood a number of people prune their bushes and trees. It is an annual practice among people who care about growing things. It is also one of those acts that an outsider, one who does not understand how growth works, almost always misunderstands, for it always looks like an act of mutilation. It appears that you are ruining the plant when, in fact, you are helping it.

We have a rosebush that hasn't been pruned for several years. When it first bloomed the roses were full and vigorous. Last summer the plant was larger than ever. The vines ranged up to the roof on a trellis I had made. I anticipated more roses than ever. But I was disappointed. The blossoms were small and scrawny. The branches had gotten too far from their roots. The plant couldn't grow a healthy blossom. It needed a good pruning.

Psalm 131 is a maintenance psalm. It is functional to the person of faith as pruning is functional to the gardener: it gets rid of that which looks good to those who don't know any better, and reduces the distance between our hearts and their roots in God.

The two things that Psalm 131 prunes away are unruly ambition and infantile dependency, what we might call getting too big for our britches and refusing to cut the apron strings. Both of these tendencies can easily be supposed to be virtues, especially by those who are not conversant with Christian ways. If we are not careful, we will be encouraging the very things that will ruin us. We are in special and constant need of expert correction. We need pruning. Jesus said, "[God] cuts off every branch of me that doesn't bear grapes. And every branch that is grape-bearing he prunes back so it will bear even more" (Jn 15:2). More than once our Lord the Spirit has used Psalm 131 to do this important work among his people. As we gain a familiarity with and an understanding of the psalm, he will be able to use it that way with us "so that we will bear even more."

Aspiration Gone Crazy

"GOD, I'm not trying to rule the roost, I don't want to be king of the mountain. I haven't meddled where I have no business or fantasized grandiose plans. I've kept my feet on the ground, I've cultivated a quiet heart."

These lines are enormously difficult for us to comprehend—not difficult to understand with our minds, for the words are all plain, but difficult to grasp with our emotions, feeling their truth. All cultures throw certain stumbling blocks in the way of those who pursue gospel realities. It is sheerest fantasy to suppose that we would have had an easier time of it as Christian believers if we were in another land or another time. It is no easier to be a Chinese Christian than to be a Spanish Christian than to be a Russian Christian than to be a Brazilian Christian than to be an American Christian—nor more difficult. The way of faith deals with realities in whatever time and whatever culture.

But there are differences from time to time and from place to place which cause special problems. For instance, when an ancient temptation or trial becomes an approved feature in the culture, a way of life that is expected and encouraged, Christians have a stumbling block put before them that is hard to recognize for what it is, for it has been made into a monument, gilded with bronze and bathed in decorative lights. It has become an object of veneration. But the plain fact is that it is right in the middle of the road of faith, obstructing discipleship. For all its fancy dress and honored position, it is still a stumbling block.

One temptation that has received this treatment in Western civilization, with some special flourishes in America, is ambition. Our culture encourages and rewards ambition without qualification. We are surrounded by a way of life in which betterment is understood as expansion, as acquisition, as fame. Everyone wants to get more. To be on top, no matter what it is the top of, is admired. There is nothing recent about the temptation. It is the oldest sin in the book, the one that got Adam thrown out of the garden and Lucifer tossed out of heaven. What is fairly new about it is the general admiration and approval that it receives.

The old story of Dr. Faustus used to be well known and appreciated as a warning. John Faustus became impatient with the limitations placed upon him in his study of law, medicine and theology. No matter how much he learned in these fields, he found he was always in the service of something greater than himself—of justice, of healing, of God. He chafed in the service and wanted out: he wanted to be in control, to break out of the limits of the finite. So he became an adept in magic, by which he was able to defy the laws of physics, the restrictions of morality and relations with God and use his knowledge for his own pleasures and purposes. In order to bring it off, though, he had to make a pact with the devil which permitted him to act for the next twenty-four years in a godlike way—living without limits, being in control instead of being in relationship, exercising power instead of practicing love. But at the end of the twenty-four years came damnation.

For generations this story has been told and retold by poets and playwrights and novelists (Goethe, Marlowe, Mann) warning people against abandoning the glorious position of being a person created in the image of God and attempting the foolhardy adventure of trying to be a god on our own. But now something alarming has happened. There have always been Faustian characters, people in the community who embarked on a way of arrogance and power; now our entire culture is Faustian. We are caught up in a way of life that, instead of delighting in finding out the meaning of God and searching out the conditions in which human qualities can best be realized, recklessly seeks ways to circumvent nature, arrogantly defies personal relationships and names God only in curses. The legend of Faustus, useful for so long in pointing out the folly of a god-defying pride, now is practically unrecognizable because the assumptions of our whole society (our educational models, our economic expectations, even our popular religion) are Faustian.

It is difficult to recognize pride as a sin when it is held up on every side as a virtue, urged as profitable and rewarded as an achievement. What is described in Scripture as the basic sin, the sin of taking things into your own hands, being your own god, grabbing what is there while you can get it, is now described as basic wisdom: improve yourself by whatever means you are able; get ahead regardless of the price, take care of me first. For a limited time it works. But at the end the devil has his due. There is damnation.

It is additionally difficult to recognize unruly ambition as a sin because it has a kind of superficial relationship to the virtue of aspiration—an impatience with mediocrity and a dissatisfaction with all things created until we are at home with the Creator, the hopeful striving for the best God has for us—the kind of thing Paul expressed: "I've got my eye on the goal, where God is beckoning us onward—to Jesus. I'm off and running, and I'm not turning back" (Phil 3:14). But if we take the energies that make for aspiration and remove God from the picture, replacing him with our own crudely sketched self-portrait, we end up with ugly arrogance. Robert Browning's fine line on aspiration, "A man's reach should exceed his grasp, or what's a heaven for?" has been distorted to "Reach for the skies and grab everything that isn't nailed down." Ambition is aspiration gone crazy. Aspiration is the channeled, creative energy that moves us to growth in Christ, shaping goals in the Spirit. Ambition takes these same energies for growth and development and uses them to make something tawdry and cheap, sweatily knocking together a Babel when we could be vacationing in Eden. Calvin comments, "Those who yield themselves up to the influence of ambition will soon lose themselves in a labyrinth of perplexity."[2]

Our lives are lived well only when they are lived on the terms of their creation, with God loving and us being loved, with God making and us being made, with God revealing and us understanding, with God commanding and us responding. Being a Christian means accepting the terms of creation, accepting God as our maker and redeemer, and growing day by day into an increasingly glorious creature in Christ, developing joy, experiencing love, maturing in peace. By the grace of Christ we experience the marvel of being made in the image of God. If we reject this way, the only alternative is to attempt the hopelessly fourth-rate, embarrassingly awkward imitation of God made in the image of men and women like us.

Both revelation and experience (Genesis and Goethe) show it to be the wrong way, and so the psalmist is wise to see it and sing, "GOD, I'm not trying to rule the roost. . . . I haven't meddled where I have no business. . . . I've kept my feet on the ground." I will not try to run my own life or the lives of others; that is God's business, I will not pretend to invent the meaning of the universe; I will accept what God has shown its meaning to be; I will not strut about demanding that I be treated as the center of my family or my neighborhood or my work, but seek to discover where I fit and do what I am good at. The soul, clamoring for attention and arrogantly parading its importance, is calmed and quieted so that it can be itself, truly.

As Content as a Child

But if we are not to be proud, clamorous, arrogant persons, what are we to be? Mousy, cringing, insecure ones? Well, not quite. Having realized the dangers of pride, the sin of thinking too much of ourselves, we are suddenly in danger of another mistake, thinking too little of ourselves. There are some who conclude that since the great Christian temptation is to try to be everything, the perfect Christian solution is to be nothing. And so we have the problem of the doormat Christian and the dishrag saint: the person upon whom everyone walks and wipes their feet, the person who is used by others to clean up the mess of everyday living and then is discarded. These people then compensate for their poor lives by weepily clinging to God, hoping to make up for the miseries of everyday life by dreaming of luxuries in heaven.

Christian faith is not neurotic dependency but childlike trust. We do not have a God who forever indulges our whims but a God whom we trust with our destinies. The Christian is not a naive, innocent infant who has no identity apart from a feeling of being comforted and protected and catered to but a person who has discovered an identity given by God which can be enjoyed best and fully in a voluntary trust in God. We do not cling to God desperately out of fear and the panic of insecurity; we come to him freely in faith and love.

Our Lord gave us the picture of the child as a model for Christian faith (Mk 10:14-16) not because of the child's helplessness but because of the child's willingness to be led, to be taught, to be blessed. God does not reduce us to a set of Pavlovian reflexes so that we mindlessly worship and pray and obey on signal; he establishes us with a dignity in which we are free to receive his word, his gifts, his grace.

The psalm shows great genius at this point and describes a relationship that is completely attractive. The translators of the Jerusalem Bible have retained the literalism of the Hebrew metaphor: "Enough for me to keep my soul tranquil and quiet like a child in its mother's arms, as content as a child that has been weaned." The last phrase, "as a child that has been weaned," creates a completely new, unguessed reality. The Christian is

> not like an infant crying loudly for his mother's breast, but like a weaned child that quietly rests by his mother's side, happy in being with her. . . . No desire now comes between him and his God; for he is sure that God knows what he needs before he asks him. And just as the child gradually breaks off the habit of regarding his mother only as a means of satisfying his own desires and learns to love her for her own sake, so the worshipper after a struggle has reached an attitude of mind in which he desires God for himself and not as a means of fulfillment of his own wishes. His life's centre of gravity has shifted. He now rests no longer in himself but in God.[3]

The transition from a sucking infant to a weaned child, from squalling baby to quiet son or daughter, is not smooth. It is stormy and noisy. It is no easy thing to quiet yourself: sooner may we calm the sea or rule the wind or tame a tiger than quiet ourselves. It is pitched battle. The baby is denied expected comforts and flies into rages or sinks into sulks. There are sobs and struggles. The infant is facing its first great sorrow and it is in sore distress. But "to the weaned child his mother is his comfort though she has denied him comfort. It is a blessed mark of growth out of spiritual infancy when we can forgo the joys which once appeared to be essential, and can find our solace in him who denies them to us."[4]

Many who have traveled this way of faith have described the transition from an infantile faith that grabs at God out of desperation to a mature faith that responds to God out of love, "like a baby content in its mother's arms." Often our conscious Christian lives do begin at points of desperation, and God, of course, does not refuse to meet our needs. Heavenly comforts break through our despair and persuade us that "all will be well and all manner of things will be well." The early stages of Christian belief are not infrequently marked with miraculous signs and exhilarations of spirit. But as discipleship continues, the sensible comforts gradually disappear. For God does not want us neurotically dependent on him but willingly trustful in him. And so he weans us. The period of infancy will not be sentimentally extended beyond what is necessary. The time of weaning is very often noisy and marked by misunderstandings: *I no longer feel like I did when I was first a Christian. Does that mean I am no longer a Christian? Has God abandoned me? Have I done something terribly wrong?*

The answer is, neither. God hasn't abandoned you and you haven't done anything wrong. You are being weaned. The apron strings have been cut. You are free to come to God or not come to him. You are, in a sense, on your own with an open invitation to listen and receive and enjoy our Lord.

The last line of the psalm addresses this quality of newly acquired freedom: "Wait, Israel, for GOD. Wait with hope. Hope now; hope always!" Choose to be with him; elect his presence; aspire to his ways; respond to his love.

The Plain Way

When Charles Spurgeon preached this psalm, he said it "is one of the shortest Psalms to read, but one of the longest to learn."[5] We are always, it seems, reeling from one side of the road to the other as we travel in the way of faith. At one turning of the road we are presented with awesome problems and terrifying emergencies. We rise to the challenge, take things into our own hands to become master of the situation, telling God, "Thank you, but get lost. We'll take care of this one ourselves." At the next turning we are overwhelmed and run in a panic to some kind of infantile religion that will solve all our problems for us, freeing us of the burden of thinking and the difficulty of choosing. We are, alternately, rebellious runaways and whining babies. Worse, we have numerous experts, so-called, encouraging us to pursue one or the other of these ways.

The experts in our society who offer to help us have a kind of general-staff mentality from which massive, top-down solutions are issued to solve our problems. Then when the solutions don't work, we get mired in the nothing-can-be-done swamp. We are first incited into being grandiose and then intimidated into being infantile. But there is another way, the plain way of quiet Christian humility. We need pruning. Cut back to our roots, we learn this psalm and discover the quietness of the weaned child, the tranquillity of maturing trust. It is such a minute psalm that many have overlooked it, but for all its brevity and lack of pretense, it is essential. For every Christian encounters problems of growth and difficulties of development.

A number of years ago Peter Marin made an incisive observation very much in the spirit of Psalm 131:

There are cultural conditions for which there are no solutions, turnings of the soul so profound and complex that no system can absorb or contain them. How could one have "solved" the Reformation? Or first-century Rome? One makes accommodations and adjustments, one dreams about the future and makes plans to save us all, but in spite of all that, because of it, what seems more important are the private independent acts that become more necessary every day: the ways we find as private persons to restore to one another the strengths we should have now—whether to make the kind of revolution we need or to survive the repression that seems likely . . . what saves us as men and women is always a kind of witness: the quality of our own acts and lives.[6]

And that is what Psalm 131 nurtures: a quality of calm confidence and quiet strength that knows the difference between unruly arrogance and faithful aspiration, knows how to discriminate between infantile dependency and childlike trust, and chooses to aspire and to trust—and to sing, "I've kept my feet on the ground, I've cultivated a quiet heart. Like a baby content in its mother's arms, my soul is a baby content."

14

OBEDIENCE

"How He Promised GOD"

O GOD, remember David,
        remember all his troubles!
And remember how he promised GOD,
    made a vow to the Strong God of Jacob,
        "I'm not going home,
        and I'm not going to bed,
        I'm not going to sleep,
        not even take time to rest,
    Until I find a home for GOD,
        a house for the Strong God of Jacob."
Remember how we got the news in Ephrathah,
    learned all about it at Jaar Meadows?
We shouted, "Let's go to the shrine dedication!
    Let's worship at God's own footstool!"
Up, GOD, enjoy your new place of quiet repose,
    you and your mighty covenant ark;
Get your priests all dressed up in justice;
    prompt your worshipers to sing this prayer:
        "Honor your servant David;
        don't disdain your anointed one."
GOD gave David his word,

he won't back out on this promise:
"One of your sons
I will set on your throne;
If your sons stay true to my Covenant
and learn to live the way I teach them,
Their sons will continue the line—
always a son to sit on your throne.

Yes—I, GOD, chose Zion,
the place I wanted for my shrine;
This will always be my home;
this is what I want, and I'm here for good.
I'll shower blessings on the pilgrims who come here,
and give supper to those who arrive hungry;
I'll dress my priests in salvation clothes;
the holy people will sing their hearts out!
Oh, I'll make the place radiant for David!
I'll fill it with light for my anointed!
I'll dress his enemies in dirty rags,
but I'll make his crown sparkle with splendor."

PSALM 132

True knowledge of God is born out of obedience.

JOHN CALVIN

An incident took place a few years ago that has acquired the force of a parable for me. I had a minor operation on my nose and was in my hospital room recovering. Even though the surgery was minor, the pain was great and I was full of misery. Late in the afternoon a man was assigned to the other bed in my room. He was to have a tonsillectomy the next day. He was young, about twenty-two years old, good-looking and friendly. He came over to me, put out his hand and said, "Hi, my name is Kelly. What happened to you?"

I was in no mood for friendly conversation, did not return the handshake, grunted my name and said that I had gotten my nose broken. He got the message that I did not want to talk, pulled the curtain between our beds and let me alone. Later in the evening his friends were visiting, and I heard him say, "There's a man in the next bed who is a prizefighter; he got his nose broken in a championship fight." He went on to embellish the story for the benefit of his friends.

Later in the evening, as I was feeling better, I said, "Kelly, you misunderstood what I said. I'm not a prizefighter. The nose was broken years ago in a basketball game, and I am just now getting it fixed."

"Well, what do you do then?"

"I'm a pastor."

"Oh," he said and turned away; I was no longer an interesting subject.

In the morning he woke me: "Peterson, Peterson—wake up."

I groggily came awake and asked what he wanted. "I want you to pray for me; I'm scared." And so, before he was taken to surgery, I went to his bedside and prayed for him.

When he was brought back a couple of hours later, a nurse came and said, "Kelly, I am going to give you an injection that should take care of any pain that you might have."

In twenty minutes or so he began to groan, "I hurt. I can't stand it. I'm going to die."

I rang for the nurse and, when she came, said, "Nurse, I don't think that shot did any good; why don't you give him another one?" She didn't acknowledge my credentials for making such a suggestion, told me curtly that she would oversee the medical care of the patient, turned on her heel and, a little abruptly I thought, left. Meanwhile Kelly continued to vent his agony.

After another half an hour he began to hallucinate, and having lost touch with reality began to shout, "Peterson, pray for me; can't you see I'm dying! Peterson, pray for me!" His shouts brought nurses and doctors and orderlies running. They held him down and quieted him with the injection that I had prescribed earlier.

The parabolic force of the incident is this: when the man was scared he wanted me to pray for him, and when the man was crazy he wanted me to pray for him, but in between, during the hours of so-called normalcy, he didn't want anything to do with a pastor. What Kelly betrayed *in extremis* is all many people know of religion: a religion to help them with their fears but that is forgotten when the fears are taken care of; a religion made of moments of craziness but that is remote and shadowy in the clear light of the sun and the routines of every day. The most religious places in the world, as a matter of fact, are not churches but battlefields and mental hospitals. You are much more likely to find passionate prayer in a foxhole than in a church pew; and you will certainly find more otherworldly visions and supernatural voices in a mental hospital than you will in a church.

Stable, Not Petrified

Nevertheless we Christians don't go to either place to nurture our faith. We don't deliberately put ourselves in places of fearful danger to evoke heartfelt prayer, and we don't put ourselves in psychiatric wards so we can be around those who clearly see visions of heaven and hell and distinctly hear the voice of God. What most Christians do is come to church, a place that is fairly safe and moderately predictable. For we have an instinct for health and sanity in our faith. We don't seek out death-defying situations, and we avoid mentally unstable teachers. But in doing that we don't get what some people seem to want very much, namely, a religion that makes us safe at all costs, certifying us as inoffensive to our neighbors and guaranteeing us as good credit risks to the banks. It would be simply awful to find that as we grew in Christ we became dull, that as we developed in discipleship we became like Anthony Trollope's Miss Thorne, whose "virtues were too numerous to describe, and not sufficiently interesting to deserve description."

We want a Christian faith that has stability but is not petrified, that has vision but is not hallucinatory. How do we get both the sense of stability and the spirit of adventure, the ballast of good health and the zest of true sanity? How do we get the adult maturity to keep our feet on the ground and retain the childlike innocence to make the leap of faith?

Psalm 132 is one of the oldest psalms in the Bible. It was included in the Songs of Ascents to develop just those aspects of life under God and in Christ which my sometime friend Kelly lacked and which we all need.

It is a psalm of David's obedience, of "how he promised GOD, made a vow to the Strong God of Jacob." The psalm shows obedience as a lively, adventurous response of faith that is rooted in historical fact and reaches into a promised hope.

Obedience with a History

The first half of Psalm 132 is the part that roots obedience in fact and keeps our feet on the ground. The psalm takes a single incident out of the past, the history of the ark of the covenant, and reminisces over it: "Remember how we got the news in Ephrathah, learned all about it at Jaar Meadows? We shouted, 'Let's go to the shrine dedication! Let's worship at God's own footstool!' Up, GOD, enjoy your new place of quiet repose, you and your mighty covenant ark."

The ark of the covenant was a box approximately forty-five inches long, twenty-seven inches broad and twenty-seven inches deep, constructed of wood and covered with gold. Its lid of solid gold was called the mercy seat. Two cherubim, angel-like figures at either end, framed the space around the central mercy seat from which God's word was heard. It had been made under the supervision of Moses (Ex 25:10-22) and was a symbol of the presence of God among his people. The ark had accompanied Israel from Sinai, through the wilderness wanderings, and had been kept at Shiloh from the time of the conquest. In a battle the ark had been captured by the enemy Philistines and was a trophy of war displayed in the Philistine cities until it became a problem to them (the story is told in 1 Samuel 4—7) and was returned to Israel, to the village of Kiriath-jearim (7:1-2), where it rested until David came to get it and place it in honor in Jerusalem, where it later became enshrined in Solomon's temple.

The history of the ark was, for the Hebrews, a kind of theological handbook. It provided an account of the presence of God among the people. Its history showed the importance of having God with you and the danger of trying to use God or carry him around. And so the ark itself was important in that it emphasized that God was with his people and that God was over and above his people (for God quite obviously was not in the box). The ark was the symbol, not the reality. When the ark was treated as a talisman, as a curio or as a magical device with which to manipulate God, everything went wrong. God cannot be contained or used.

The psalm does not retell this history, it only remembers the history. There is only enough here to trigger the historical memories of the people. For the rich symbolism of the ark was everyday stuff to them. Its extensive and intricate history was common knowledge, much as the story of Jesus is to Christians. With promptings from the psalm, the story would come alive for them again, especially the part telling of the time when David rediscovered the ark in an obscure village and determined to set it at the center of Israelite life, restoring an old unity to the life of the people of God in adoration and worship. "Remember how we got the news in Ephrathah, learned all about it at Jaar Meadows." News had come to David of where the ark was; he vowed to get it and was obedient to his vow. He gathered his people to himself and said: "Let's go to the shrine dedication! Let's worship at God's own footstool!" He went to the ark and brought it up to Jerusalem in festive parade: "Up, GOD, enjoy your new place of quiet repose, you and your mighty covenant ark; / Get your priests all dressed up in justice, prompt your worshipers to sing . . ." As the song was sung, we are told, "David danced with great abandon before GOD. The whole country was with him as he brought the Ark of God with shouts and trumpet blasts" (2 Sam 6:14-15).

As this old ark song is resung now by the people of God on pilgrimage, historical memories are revived and relived: there is a vast, rich reality of obedience beneath the feet of disciples. They are not the first persons to ascend these slopes on their way of obedience to God, and they will not be the last. Up these same roads, along these same paths, the ark had been carried, accompanied by a determined and expectant people. It had been carried in both good and bad ways. They would remember the time they carried it in panic ("I'm scared! Pray for me!"), superstitiously as a secret weapon against the Philistines. *That* ended in calamity. They would also remember the Davidic parade of awed adoration and dancing celebration as obedience was turned into worship. Christians tramp well-worn paths: obedience has a history.

This history is important, for without it we are at the mercy of whims. Memory is a databank we use to evaluate our position and make decisions. With a biblical memory we have two thousand years of experience from which to make the off-the-cuff responses that are required each day in the life of faith. If we are going to live adequately and maturely as the people of God, we need more data to work from than our own experience can give us.

What would we think of a pollster who issued a definitive report on how the American people felt about a new television special, if we discovered later that he had interviewed only one person who had seen only ten minutes of the program? We would dismiss the conclusions as frivolous. Yet that is exactly the kind of evidence that too many Christians accept as the final truth about many much more important matters—matters such as answered prayer, God's judgment, Christ's forgiveness, eternal salvation. The only person they consult is themselves, and the only experience they evaluate is the most recent ten minutes. But we need other experiences, the community of experience of brothers and sisters in the church, the centuries of experience provided by our biblical ancestors. A Christian who has David in his bones, Jeremiah in his bloodstream, Paul in his fingertips and Christ in his heart will know how much and how little value to put on his own momentary feelings and the experience of the past week.

To remain willfully ignorant of Abraham wandering in the desert, the Hebrews enslaved in Egypt, David battling the Philistines, Jesus arguing with the Pharisees and Paul writing to the Corinthians is like saying, "I refuse to remember that when I kicked that black dog last week he bit my leg." If I don't remember it, in the next fit of anger I will kick him again and get bitten again. Biblical history is a good memory for what doesn't work. It is also a good memory for what does work—like remembering what you put in the soup that made it taste so good so you can repeat and enjoy the recipe on another day, or remembering the shortcut through the city to the ocean that saved you from being tied up in traffic and got you to the beach two hours earlier.

A Christian with a defective memory has to start everything from scratch and spends far too much of his or her time backtracking, repairing, starting over. A Christian with a good memory avoids repeating old sins, knows the easiest way through complex situations and instead of starting over each day continues what was begun in Adam. Psalm 132 activates faith's memory so that obedience will be sane. "Each act of obedience by the Christian is a modest proof, unequivocal for all its imperfection, of the reality of what he attests."[1]

Hope: A Race Toward God's Promises

But Psalm 132 doesn't just keep our feet on the ground, it also gets them off the ground. Not only is it a solid foundation for the past, it is a daring leap into the future. For obedience is not a stodgy plodding in the ruts of religion, it is a hopeful race toward God's promises. The second half of the psalm has a propellant quality to it. The psalmist is not an antiquarian reveling in the past for its own sake but a traveler using what he knows of the past to get to where he is going—to God.

For all its interest in history the Bible never refers to the past as "the good old times." The past is not, for the person of faith, a restored historical site that we tour when we are on vacation; it is a field that we plow and harrow and plant and fertilize and work for a harvest.

The second half of Psalm 132 takes seriously what God said to David and how David responded (matters that are remembered in the ark narrative) and uses them to make a vision of the reality that is in the future of faith: "I'll shower blessings on the pilgrims who come here, and give supper to those who arrive hungry; I'll dress my priests in salvation clothes; the holy people will sing their hearts out! Oh, I'll make the place radiant for David! I'll fill it with light for my anointed! I'll dress his enemies in dirty rags, but I'll make his crown sparkle with splendor." All the verb tenses are future. Obedience is fulfilled by hope.

Now none of these hopes is unrelated to or detached from actual history: each develops from what a person with a good memory knows happened.

"I'll shower blessings on the pilgrims who come here, and give supper to those who arrive hungry." The devout mind goes back to those years in the wilderness when God gave water from the rock, manna from the ground and quail from the skies, and fashions a hope for abundant, eternal providence.

"I'll dress my priests in salvation clothes; the holy people will sing their hearts out!" No other people knew so much of salvation as Israel. The priests renewed the knowledge and applied it to daily

life at every gathering of worship—occasions that were always
marked with joy—renewing the life of redemption. Has any
other people had such a good time with their faith as Israel?
From Moses' song at the edge of the Red Sea with Miriam and
the women accompanying with tambourines, to the victorious
trumpets that shook and finally tumbled the walls of Jericho, to
the robust hymns of David that we continue to sing in our
churches today, the joy has overflowed.

*"Oh, I'll make the place radiant for David! I'll fill it with light
for my anointed."* Light—radiant light!—pervades Scripture and
creation as a sign of God's presence. The hope is that its brightness will provide light for the path of the one who represents
God's presence, a light we now identify with revelation in Scripture and in Christ.

*"I'll dress his enemies in dirty rags, but I'll make his crown spar-
kle with splendor."* The shame of God's enemies and the glory of
God's king will finally be decisive. The triumph will be complete. Evil will lie sprawling in defeat, righteousness will flourish
in victory. That is an agenda that hope writes for obedience.

Psalm 132 cultivates a hope that gives wings to obedience, a
hope that is consistent with the reality of what God has done in the
past but is not confined to it. All the expectations listed in Psalm
132 have their origin in an accurately remembered past. But they
are not simply repetitions of the past projected into the future.
They are developments out of it, with new features of their own.

Christians who master Psalm 132 will be protected from one
danger, at least, that is ever a threat to obedience: the danger
that we should reduce Christian existence to ritually obeying a
few commandments that are congenial to our temperament and
convenient to our standard of living. It gives us, instead, a vision
into the future so that we can see what is right before us. If we
define the nature of our lives by the mistake of the moment or

the defeat of the hour or the boredom of the day, we will define it wrongly. We need roots in the past to give obedience ballast and breadth; we need a vision of the future to give obedience direction and goal. And they must be connected. There must be an organic unity between them.

If we never learn how to do this—extend the boundaries of our lives beyond the dates enclosed by our birth and death and acquire an understanding of God's way as something larger and more complete than the anecdotes in our private diaries—we will forever be missing the point of things by making headlines out of something that ought to be tucked away on page 97 in section C of the newspaper or putting into the classified ads something that should be getting a full-page color advertisement—mistaking a sore throat for a descent into hell. ("Peterson, pray for me!") For Christian faith cannot be comprehended by examining an Instamatic flash picture which has caught a pose of beauty or absurdity, ecstasy or terror; it is a full revelation of a vast creation and a grandly consummated redemption. Obedience is doing what God tells us to do in it.

The Strength to Stand, the Willingness to Leap

In such ways Psalm 132 cultivates the memory and nurtures the hope that lead to mature obedience. It protects us from a religion that is ignorant of the ways of God and so keeps us prey to every fear that thrusts itself upon us. It guards us from a religion run riot with fantasies and nightmares because it has gotten disassociated from the promises of God. It develops a strong sense of continuity with the past and a surging sense of exploration into the future. It is the kind of thing we sing to stay normal without becoming dull, to walk upright in the middle of the road without getting stuck in a long rut of mediocrity. Its words prod us to reach into the future without losing touch with daily reality. Its rhythms stimulate us to new adventures in the Spirit without making us lunatics. For Christian living demands that we keep our feet on the ground; it also asks us to make a leap of faith. A Christian who stays put is no better than a statue. A person who leaps about constantly is under suspicion of being not a man but a jumping jack. What we require is obedience—the strength to stand and the willingness to leap, and the sense to know when to do which. Which is exactly what we get when an accurate memory of God's ways is combined with a lively hope in his promises.

15

COMMUNITY

"Like Costly Anointing Oil Flowing Down Head & Beard"

How wonderful, how beautiful,
when brothers and sisters get along!
It's like costly anointing oil
flowing down head and beard,
Flowing down Aaron's beard,
flowing down the collar of his priestly robes.
It's like the dew on Mount Hermon
flowing down the slopes of Zion.
Yes, that's where GOD commands the blessing,
ordains eternal life.

PSALM 133

All actual life is encounter.

MARTIN BUBER

W hether we like it or not, the moment we confess Jesus Christ as our Lord and Savior, that is, from the time we become a Christian, we are at the same time a member of the Christian church—even if we do not permit our name to be placed on a church roll, even if we refuse to identify ourselves with a particular congregation and share responsibilities with them, even if we absent ourselves from the worship of a congregation. Our membership in the church is a corollary of our faith in Christ. We can no more be a Christian and have nothing to do with the church than we can be a person and not be in a family. Membership in the church is a basic spiritual fact for those who confess Christ as Lord. It is not an option for those Christians who happen by nature to be more gregarious than others. It is part of the fabric of redemption.

There are Christians, of course, who never put their names down on a membership list; there are Christians who refuse to respond to the call to worship each Sunday; there are Christians who say, "I love God but I hate the church." But they are members all the same, whether they like it or not, whether they acknowledge it or not. For God never makes private, secret salvation deals with people. His relationships with us are personal, true; intimate, yes; but private, no. We are a family in Christ. When we become Christians, we are among brothers and sisters in faith. No Christian is an only child.

But of course, the fact that we are a family of faith does not mean we are one big happy family. The people we encounter as brothers and sisters in faith are not always nice people. They do not stop being sinners the moment they begin believing in Christ. They don't suddenly metamorphose into brilliant conversationalists, exciting companions and glowing inspirations. Some of them are cranky, some of them dull and others (if the truth must be spoken) a drag. But at the same time our Lord tells us that they are brothers and sisters in faith. If God is my Father, then this is my family.

So the question is not "Am I going to be a part of a community of faith?" but "How am I going to live in this community of faith?" God's children do different things. Some run away from it and pretend that the family doesn't exist. Some move out and get an apartment on their own from which they return to make occasional visits, nearly always showing up for the parties and bringing a gift to show that they really do hold the others in fond regard. And some would never dream of leaving but cause others to dream it for them, for they are always criticizing what is served at the meals, quarreling with the way the housekeeping is done and complaining that the others in the family are either ignoring or taking advantage of them. And some determine to find out what God has in mind by placing them in this community called a church, learn how to function in it harmoniously and joyously, and develop the maturity that is able to share and exchange God's grace with those who might otherwise be viewed as nuisances.

Not Like Paying Taxes

Psalm 133 presents what we are after: "How wonderful, how beautiful, when brothers and sisters get along!" The psalm puts into song what is said and demonstrated throughout Scripture and church: community is essential. Scripture knows nothing of the solitary Christian. People of faith are always members of a

community. Creation itself was not complete until there was
community, Adam needing Eve before humanity was whole.
God never works with individuals in isolation, but always with
people in community.

This is the biblical datum, and that with which we must begin. Jesus worked with twelve disciples and lived with them in
community. The church was formed when one hundred twenty
people were "all together" in one place (Acts 2:1 and again
5:12). When some early Christians were dropping out of the
community and pursuing private interests, a pastor wrote to
them urging them to nurture their precious gift of community,
"not avoiding worshiping together as some do but spurring
each other on, especially as we see the big Day approaching"
(Heb 10:25). The Bible knows nothing of a religion defined by
what a person does inwardly in the privacy of thought or feeling,
or apart from others on lonely retreat. When Jesus was asked
what the great commandment was, he said, "Love the Lord
your God with all your passion and prayer and intelligence," and
then immediately, before anyone could go off and make a private religion out of it ("I come to the garden alone"), riveted it
to another: "There is a second to set alongside it: 'Love others
as well as you love yourself' " (Mt 22:34-40).

Christians make this explicit in their act of worship each week
by gathering as a community: other people are unavoidably
present. As we come to declare our love for God, we must face
the unlovely and lovely fellow sinners whom God loves and commands us to love. This must not be treated as something to put
up with, one of the inconvenient necessities of faith in the way
that paying taxes is an inconvenient consequence of living in a secure and free nation. It is not only necessary; it is desirable that
our faith have a social dimension, a human relationship: "How
wonderful, how beautiful, when brothers and sisters get along!"

For centuries this psalm was sung on the road as throngs of people made the ascent to Jerusalem for festival worship. Our imaginations readily reconstruct those scenes. How great to have everyone sharing a common purpose, traveling a common path, striving toward a common goal, that path and purpose and goal being God. How much better than making the long trip alone: "How good, how delightful it is for all to live together like brothers" (JB).

Two Ways to Avoid Community

But if living in community is necessary and desirable, it is also enormously difficult.[1] There is a clue to the nature of the difficulty in the phrase "when brothers and sisters get along."

Most Christians have some firsthand experience of what it means to live with brothers and sisters. Brothers fight. And sisters fight. The first story in the Bible about brothers living together is the story of Cain and Abel. And it is a murder story. Significantly, their fight was a religious fight, a quarrel over which of them God loved best. The story of Joseph and his brothers follows a few pages later, in which Joseph, envied by the rest, is sold into Egypt as a slave. Miriam and Aaron quarreled with their brother Moses. David and his brothers fare no better and add to the evidence of discord. Even Jesus and his brothers are evidence of disharmony rather than peace. The one picture we have of them shows the brothers misunderstanding Jesus and trying to drag him away from his messianic work because they are convinced that he is crazy.

Those who have acquired their knowledge of human relationships by reading psychology books instead of the Bible find the case histories on this subject under the chapter entitled "Sibling Rivalry." But most of what is there is only a footnote to what Scripture says: children fight a lot; each brother is quick to take offense if he doesn't get his own way; each sister wants a major share of the parents' attention.

Children are ordinarily so full of their own needs and wants that they look at a brother or sister not as an ally but as a competitor. If there is only one pork chop on the plate and three of us who want it, I will look at my brother and sister not as delightful dinner companions but as difficult rivals. Much of the literature of the world (novels, plays, poetry) documents this: living together like brothers and sisters means, in actual practice, endless squabbles, murderous quarrels and angry arguments. And so if we are going to sing "How wonderful, how beautiful, when brothers and sisters get along," we will not do it by being left to ourselves, following our natural bent. If we do, we will only get into a big fight, and the only wonderful thing about it will be the pleasure the spectators get in watching us bloody each other's noses.

Living together in a way that evokes the glad song of Psalm 133 is one of the great and arduous tasks before Christ's people. Nothing requires more attention and energy. It is easier to do almost anything else. It is far easier to deal with people as problems to be solved than to have anything to do with them in community. If a person can be isolated from the family (from husband, from wife, from parents, from children, from neighbors) and then be professionally counseled, advised and guided without the complications of all of those relationships, things are very much simpler. But if such practices are engaged in systematically, they become an avoidance of community. Christians are a community of people who are visibly together at worship but who remain in relationship through the week in witness and service. "In the beginning is the relation."[2]

Another common way to avoid community is to turn the church into an institution. In this way people are treated not on the basis of personal relationships but in terms of impersonal functions. Goals are set that will catch the imagination of the largest numbers of people; structures are developed that will accomplish the goal through planning and organization. Organizational planning and institutional goals become the criteria by which the community is defined and evaluated. In the process the church becomes less and less a community, that is, people who pay attention to each other, "brothers and sisters," and more and more a collectivism of "contributing units."

Every community of Christians is imperiled when either of these routes are pursued: the route of defining others as problems to be solved, the way one might repair an automobile; the route of lumping persons together in terms of economic ability or institutional effectiveness, the way one might run a bank. Somewhere between there is community—a place where each person is taken seriously, learns to trust others, depend on others, be compassionate with others, rejoice with others. "How wonderful, how beautiful, when brothers and sisters get along!"

Each Other's Priest

There are two poetic images in Psalm 133 that are rich with insights in the work of encouraging and shaping a good and delightful life together in Christ. The first image describes community as "costly anointing oil flowing down head and beard, / Flowing down Aaron's beard, flowing down the collar of his priestly robes."

The picture comes from Exodus 29, where instructions are given for the ordination of Aaron and other priests. After sacrifices were prepared, Aaron was to be dressed in the priestly vestments. Then this direction is given: "You shall take the anointing oil, and pour it on his head and anoint him. . . . Thus you shall ordain Aaron and his sons" (Ex 29:7, 9 RSV).

Oil, throughout Scripture, is a sign of God's presence, a symbol of the Spirit of God. Oil glistens, picks up the warmth of sunlight, softens the skin, perfumes the person. (Gerard Manley Hopkins, extolling God's grandeur in creation, uses a similar image in his line "It gathers to a greatness, like the ooze of oil crushed.")[3] There is a quality of warmth and ease in God's community which contrasts with the icy coldness and hard surfaces of people who jostle each other in mobs and crowds.

But more particularly here the oil is an anointing oil, marking the person as a priest. Living together means seeing the oil flow over the head, down the face, through the beard, onto the shoulders of the other—and when I see that I know that my brother, my sister, is my priest. When we see the other as God's anointed, our relationships are profoundly affected.

No one has realized this more perceptively in our time than Dietrich Bonhoeffer. He wrote, "Not what a man is in himself as a Christian, his spirituality and piety, constitutes the basis of our community. What determines our brotherhood is what that man is by reason of Christ. Our community with one another consists solely in what Christ has done to both of us."[4] And what Christ has done is anoint us with his Spirit. We are set apart for service to one another. We mediate to one another the mysteries of God. We represent to one another the address of God. We are priests who speak God's Word and share Christ's sacrifice.

> The Christian needs another Christian who speaks God's Word to him. He needs him again and again when he becomes uncertain and discouraged, for by himself he cannot help himself without belying the truth. He needs his brother man as a bearer and proclaimer of the divine word of salvation. He needs his brother solely because of Jesus Christ. The Christ in his own heart is weaker than the Christ in the word of his brother; his own heart is uncertain, his brother's is sure.[5]

In the second image, the community is "like the dew on Mount Hermon flowing down the slopes of Zion." Hermon, the highest mountain in that part of the world, rises to a height of over nine thousand feet in the Lebanon range, north of Israel. Anyone who has slept overnight in high alpine regions knows how heavy the dew is at such altitudes. When you wake in the morning, you are drenched. This heavy dew, which was characteristic of each new dawn on the high slopes of Hermon, is extended by the imagination to the hills of Zion—a copious dew, fresh and nurturing in the drier, barren Judean country. The alpine dew communicates a sense of morning freshness, a feeling of fertility, a clean anticipation of growth.

Important in any community of faith is an ever-renewed expectation in what God is doing with our brothers and sisters in the faith. We refuse to label the others as one thing or another. We refuse to predict our brother's behavior, our sister's growth. Each person in the community is unique; each is specially loved and particularly led by the Spirit of God. How can I presume to make conclusions about anyone? How can I pretend to know your worth or your place? Margaret Mead, who made learned and passionate protests against the ways modern culture flattens out and demoralizes people, wrote, "No recorded cultural system has ever had enough different expectations to match all the children who were born within it."[6]

A community of faith flourishes when we view each other with this expectancy, wondering what God will do today in this one, in that one. When we are in a community with those Christ loves and redeems, we are constantly finding out new things about them. They are new persons each morning, endless in their possibilities. We explore the fascinating depths of their friendship, share the secrets of their quest. It is impossible to be bored in such a community, impossible to feel alienated among such people.

The oil flowing down Aaron's beard communicates warm, priestly relationship. The dew descending down Hermon's slopes communicates fresh and expectant newness. Oil and dew. The two things that make life together delightful.

Rousing Good Fellowship
The last line of the psalm concludes that the good and delightful life together is where "GOD commands the blessing, ordains eternal life."

Christians are always attempting and never quite succeed at getting a picture of the life everlasting. When we try to imagine it, we only banalize it. And then, having scrawled an uninteresting and amateurish sketch using the paint pots of an impoverished faith, we announce that we are not so sure we want to spend eternity in a place like that. Maybe we would prefer the rousing good fellowship of hell. Psalm 133 throws out just a hint of heaven (a hint that is expanded into a grand vision in Revelation 4—5), turning that on its head: the rousing good fellowship is in heaven.

Where relationships are warm and expectancies fresh, we are already beginning to enjoy the life together that will be completed in our life everlasting. Which means that heaven is like nothing quite so much as a good party. Assemble in your imagination all the friends you enjoy being with most, the companions who evoke the deepest joy, your most stimulating relationships, the most delightful of shared experiences, the people with whom you feel completely alive—*that* is a hint at heaven, "for there GOD commands the blessing, ordains eternal life."

April 9, 1945
One of the best, maybe *the* best, book written in the twentieth century on the meaning of living together as a family of faith is

Life Together by Dietrich Bonhoeffer. The book begins with the words of the psalm: "Behold, how good and how pleasant it is for brethren to live together in unity!" (NKJV). The text was with Bonhoeffer all his life. His first publication, a doctoral dissertation at age twenty-one, was titled "The Communion of the Saints." His book *The Cost of Discipleship* has been a handbook to a vast company of Christians on pilgrimage. During the Nazi years he led a fugitive community of seminarians, living with them in a daily quest to discover for themselves the meaning of being a family of faith in Christ and training them in the pastoral ministries that would lead others into that fellowship of a common life. It was during this period that he wrote *Life Together.*

During the last years of the Third Reich he was imprisoned by Adolf Hitler. But even then prison walls did not separate him from his brothers and sisters in Christ. He prayed for them and wrote letters to them, deepening the experience of community in Christ. And then he was killed. Even as his life had been an exploration of the first line of Psalm 133, his death was an exposition of the last line: "GOD commands the blessing, ordains eternal life."

The time was April 9th, 1945. The prison doctor at Flossenburg wrote this report: "On the morning of the day, some time between five and six o'clock the prisoners . . . were led out of their cells and the verdicts read to them. Through the half-open door of a room in one of the huts I saw Pastor Bonhoeffer, still in his prison clothes, kneeling in fervent prayer to the Lord his God. The devotion and evident conviction of being heard that I saw in the prayer of this intensely captivating man, moved me to the depths." So the morning came. Now the prisoners were ordered to strip. They were led down a little flight of steps under the trees to the secluded place of execution. There was a pause. . . . Naked under the scaffold in the sweet spring woods, Bonhoeffer knelt

for the last time to pray. Five minutes later, his life was ended.
. . . Three weeks later Hitler committed suicide. In another
month the Third Reich had fallen. All Germany was in chaos and
communications were impossible. No one knew what had happened to Bonhoeffer. His family waited in anguished uncertainty
in Berlin. The report of his death was first received in Geneva and
then telegraphed to England. On July 27th his aged parents, as
was their custom, turned on their radio to listen to the broadcast
from London. A memorial service was in progress. The triumphant measures of Vaughan Williams' "For All the Saints" rolled
out loud and solemn from many hundred voices. Then a single
German was speaking in English, "We are gathered here in the
presence of God to make thankful remembrance of the life and
work of his servant Dietrich Bonhoeffer, who gave his life in faith
and obedience to His holy word."[7]

In such a way one man showed in his life and death, even as
we can in the communities we live in and lead, the rich and continuing truths of Psalm 133: "How wonderful, how beautiful,
when brothers and sisters get along. . . . That's where GOD
commands the blessing, ordains eternal life."

16

BLESSING

"Lift Your Praising Hands"

Come, bless GOD,
all you servants of GOD!
You priests of GOD, posted to the nightwatch
in GOD's shrine,
Lift your praising hands to the Holy Place,
and bless GOD.
In turn, may GOD of Zion bless you—
GOD who made heaven and earth!

PSALM 134

Not seldom in this life, when, on the right side,
fortune's favorites sail close by us, we, though all adroop before,
catch somewhat of the rushing breeze,
and joyfully feel our bagging sails fill out.

HERMAN MELVILLE

M onths of struggle, of strategy, of sacrifice all paid off in a landslide victory for President Richard Nixon in 1972. On election night his aide Charles Colson was in the place he had always wanted to be. The picture Colson draws of that night contains three figures: chief of staff H. R. Haldeman, arrogant and sullen; Nixon, restlessly gulping scotch; and Colson, feeling let down, deflated, "a deadness inside me." Three men at the power pinnacle of the world, and not a single note of joy discernible in the room. "If someone had peered in on us that night from some imaginary peephole in the ceiling of the President's office, what a curious sight it would have been: a victorious President, grumbling over words he would grudgingly say to his fallen foe; his chief of staff angry, surly, and snarling; and the architect of his political strategy sitting in numbed stupor."[1]

The experience is not uncommon. We work hard for something, get it and then find we don't want it. We struggle for years to get to the top and find life there thoroughly boring. Colson writes, "Being part of electing a President was the fondest ambition of my life. For three long years I had committed everything I had, every ounce of energy to Richard Nixon's cause. Nothing else mattered. We had had no time together as a family, no social life, no vacations."[2] And then, having in his hands what he had set out to gain, he found he couldn't enjoy it.

For some the goal is an academic degree; for some a career position; for some a certain standard of living; for some acquiring a possession, getting married, having a child, landing a job, visiting a country, meeting a celebrity. But having gotten what we had always wanted, we find we have not gotten what we wanted at all. We are less fulfilled than ever, and are conscious only of "a deadness inside me."

Stand, Stoop, Stay

In Psalm 120, the first of the Songs of Ascents, we saw the theme of *repentance* developed. The word in Hebrew is *těshubah,* a turning away from the world and a turning toward God—the initial move in a life-goal set on God. It was addressed to the person at the crossroads, inviting each of us to make the decision to set out on the way of faith. Each of the psalms following has described a part of what takes place along this pilgrim way among people who have turned to God and follow him in Christ. We have discovered in these psalms beautiful lines, piercing insights, dazzling truths, stimulating words. We have found that the world in which these psalms are sung is a world of adventure and challenge, of ardor and meaning. We have realized that while there are certainly difficulties in the way of faith, it cannot by any stretch of the imagination be called dull. It requires everything that is in us; it enlists all our desires and abilities; it gathers our total existence into its songs. But when we get to where we are going, what then? What happens at the end of faith? What takes place when we finally arrive? Will we be disappointed?

Psalm 134, the final Song of Ascents, provides the evidence. The way of discipleship that begins in an act of repentance *(těshubah)* concludes in a life of praise *(běrakah).* It doesn't take long to find the key word and controlling thought in the psalm: *bless* God, *bless* God, God *bless* you.

There are two words which are translated "blessed" in our Bibles. One is *'ashre,* which describes the having-it-all-together sense of well-being that comes when we are living in tune with creation and redemption. It is what Psalm 1 announces and what Psalm 128 describes. It is what we experience when God blesses us. The word in Hebrew "is used only of men, never of God, [and] in the NT there are only two instances in which it is used of God (*makarios* in 1 Tim 1:11; 6:15)."[3] The other word is *bĕrakah*. It describes what God does to us and among us: he enters into covenant with us, he pours out his own life for us, he shares the goodness of his Spirit, the vitality of his creation, the joys of his redemption. He empties himself among us, and we get what he is. That is *blessing*. When the first word is *tĕshubah,* the last word is *bĕrakah*.

God gets down on his knees among us, gets on our level and shares himself with us. He does not reside afar off and send us diplomatic messages; he kneels among us. That posture is characteristic of God. The discovery and realization of this is what defines what we know of God as *good* news—God shares himself generously and graciously. "Whichever form the blessing takes, it implies an exchange of the contents of the soul."[4] God enters into our need, he anticipates our goals, he "gets into our skin" and understands us better than we do ourselves. Everything we learn about God through Scripture and in Christ tells us that he knows what it is like to change a diaper for the thirteenth time in the day, to see a report over which we have worked long and carefully gather dust on somebody's desk for weeks and weeks, to find our teaching treated with scorn and indifference by children and youth, to discover that the integrity and excellence of our work has been overlooked and the shoddy duplicity of another's rewarded with a promotion.

A book on God has for its title *The God Who Stands, Stoops and Stays*. That summarizes the posture of blessing: God stands—he is foundational and dependable; God stoops—he

kneels to our level and meets us where we are; God stays—he
sticks with us through hard times and good, sharing his life with
us in grace and peace.

And because God blesses us, we bless God. We respond with
that which we have received. We participate in the process that
God has initiated and continues. We who are blessed, bless. When
the word is used for what people do, it has, in Scripture, the sense
of "praise and gratitude for blessing received."[5] The people who
learn what it is like to receive the blessing, persons who travel the
way of faith experiencing the ways of grace in all kinds of weather
and over every kind of terrain, become good at blessing. In Israel
this became "the distinctive expression of the practice of religion."[6] In Judaism to this day all forms of prayer that begin with
praise of God are called *bĕrakoth*—that is, blessings.[7]

An Invitation and a Command

There is no better summarizing and concluding word in all of
Scripture than *blessing*. It describes what we most prize in God's
dealing with us and what is most attractive when we evaluate
our way of living. Every act of worship concludes with a benediction. Psalm 134 features the word in a form that might be
called an invitational command: "Come, bless GOD. . . . Lift
your praising hands . . . and bless GOD."

The persons who first sang this song had been traveling, literally, the roads that led to Jerusalem. Now they had arrived and
were at the temple to worship God in festival celebration. Some
would have been on the road for days, some for weeks, in some
instances perhaps for months. Now they were at the end of the
road. What would happen? What would they feel? What would
they do? Would there be the "deadness inside"?

Read one way, the sentence is an invitation: "Come, bless
GOD." The great promise of being in Jerusalem is that all may

join in the rich temple worship. You are welcome now to do it. Come and join in. Don't be shy. Don't hold back. Did you have a fight with your spouse on the way? That's all right. You are here now. Bless God. Did you quarrel with your neighbor while making the trip? Forget it. You are here now. Bless God. Did you lose touch with your children while coming and aren't sure just where they are now? Put that aside for the moment. They have their own pilgrimage to make. You are here. Bless God. Are you ashamed of the feelings you had while traveling? the grumbling you indulged in? the resentment you harbored? Well, it wasn't bad enough to keep you from arriving, and now that you are here, bless God. Are you embarrassed at the number of times you quit and had to have someone pick you up and carry you along? No matter. You are here. Bless God.

The sentence is an invitation; it is also a command. Having arrived at the place of worship, will we now sit around and tell stories about the trip? Having gotten to the big city, will we spend our time here as tourists, visiting the bazaars, window shopping and trading? Having gotten Jerusalem checked off our list of things to do, will we immediately begin looking for another challenge, another holy place to visit? Will the temple be a place to socialize, receive congratulations from others on our achievement, a place to share gossip and trade stories, a place to make business contacts that will improve our prospects back home? But that is not why you made the trip: bless God. You are here because God blessed you. Now you bless God.

Our stories may be interesting, but they are not the point. Our achievements may be marvelous, but they are not germane. Our curiosity may be understandable, but it is not relevant. Bless the Lord. "When the Complete arrives, our incompletes will be canceled" (1 Cor 13:10). Bless God. Do that for which you were created and redeemed; lift your voices in gratitude; enter into the community of praise and prayer that anticipates the final consummation of faith in heaven. Bless God.

Feelings Don't Run the Show

We are invited to bless the Lord; we are commanded to bless the Lord. And then someone says, "But I don't feel like it. And I won't be a hypocrite. I can't bless God if I don't feel like blessing God. It wouldn't be honest."

The biblical response to that is "Lift up your praising hands to the Holy Place, and bless GOD!" You can lift up your hands regardless of how you feel; it is a simple motor movement. You may not be able to command your heart, but you can command your arms. Lift your arms in blessing; just maybe your heart will get the message and be lifted up also in praise. We are psychosomatic beings; body and spirit are intricately interrelated. Go through the motions of blessing God and your spirit will pick up the cue and follow along. "For why do men lift their hands when they pray? Is it not that their hearts may be raised at the same time to God?"[8]

It isn't quite the same thing, and there are many differences in detail, but there is a broad similarity between the directions in the psalm and the contemporary movement known as "behavior modification"—which in a rough-and-ready way means that you can act yourself into a new way of being. Find the right things to do, practice the actions, and other things will follow. "Lift up your praising hands to the Holy Place, and bless GOD." Act your gratitude; pantomime your thanks; you will become that which you do.

Many think that the only way to change your behavior is to first change your feelings. We take a pill to alter our moods so that we won't kick the dog. We turn on music to soothe our emotions so that our conversation will be less abrasive. But there is an older wisdom that puts it differently: by changing our behavior we can change our feelings.

One person says, "I don't like that man; therefore I will not speak to him. When and if my feelings change, I will speak." Another says, "I don't like that person; therefore I am going to speak to him." The person, surprised at the friendliness, cheerfully responds and suddenly friendliness is shared. One person says, "I don't feel like worshiping; therefore I am not going to church. I will wait till I feel like it and then I will go." Another says, "I don't feel like worshiping; therefore I will go to church and put myself in the way of worship." In the process she finds herself blessed and begins, in turn, to bless.

Most probably the people who were first addressed by this command were the professional leaders of worship in the Jerusalem temple, the Levites ("you priests of GOD, posted to the nightwatch in GOD's shrine"). They worked in shifts around the clock during festival time, and through the night some of them were always on duty. The great danger in those hours was that the worship might be listless and slovenly. What can you expect at three o'clock in the morning? "No excuses," says the psalm singer, "your feelings might be flat, but you can control your muscles: lift up your hands."

Humphrey Bogart once defined a professional as a person who "did a better job when he didn't feel like it." That goes for a Christian too. Feelings don't run the show. There is a reality deeper than our feelings. Live by that. Eric Routley thinks that, colloquially, to bless means to "speak well of."[9] The Lord has spoken well of you; now you speak well of him.

Taking God Seriously but Not Ourselves

It is as easy to find instances of people who bless in Christian ranks as it is to find examples of people who curse in the world's.

Karl Barth is one of my favorites. He is one of the great theologians of all time, but the really attractive thing about him is that he was a man who blessed God. His mind was massive, his learning immense, his theological industry simply staggering. He wrote a six-million-word, seven-thousand-page, twelve-volume dogmatics plus forty or fifty other books and several hundred learned articles. Impressive as that is, what is far more impressive, to me at least, is what he called *Dankbarkeit*. Gratitude. Always and everywhere we are aware that Barth was responding to God's grace; there is a chuckle rumbling underneath his most serious prose; there is a twinkle on the edges of his eyes—always. He never took himself seriously and always took God seriously, and therefore he was full of cheerfulness, exuberant with blessing. Speaking of his own work as a theologian he said, "The theologian who has no joy in his work is not a theologian at all. Sulky faces, morose thoughts and boring ways of speaking are intolerable in this science."[10]

Once Barth was on a bus in Basel, the Swiss city in which he lived and taught for many years. A man came and sat beside him, a tourist. Barth struck up a conversation, "You are a visitor, yes? And what do you want to see in our city?"

The man said, "I would like to see the great theologian Karl Barth. Do you know him?"

"Oh, yes," said Barth, "I shave him every morning." The man went away satisfied, telling his friends that he had met Barth's barber.

Because he refused to take himself seriously and decided to take God seriously, Barth burdened neither himself nor those around him with the gloomy, heavy seriousness of ambition or pride or sin or self-righteousness. Instead, the lifting up of hands, the brightness of blessing.

Charles Dickens described one of his characters as a person "who called her rigidity religion."[11] We find that kind of thing far too often, but, thankfully, we do not find it in Scripture. In Scripture we find Jesus concluding his parable of the lost sheep with the words "Count on it—there's more joy in heaven over one sinner's rescued life than over ninety-nine good people in no need of rescue" (Lk 15:7). Not relief, not surprise, not self-satisfied smugness. And certainly not the "deadness inside me." But joy.

Blessing is at the end of the road. And that which is at the end of the road influences everything that takes place along the road. The end shapes the means. As Catherine of Siena said, "All the way to heaven is heaven." A joyful end requires a joyful means. Bless the Lord.

The Chief End

I have a friend who is dean in a theological seminary where men and women are being trained to be pastors. Sometimes he calls one of these people into his office and says something like this: "You have been around here for several months now, and I have had an opportunity to observe you. You get good grades, seem to take your calling to ministry seriously, work hard and have clear goals. But I don't detect any joy. You don't seem to have any pleasure in what you are doing. And I wonder if you should not reconsider your calling into ministry. For if a pastor is not in touch with joy, it will be difficult to teach or preach convincingly that the news is good. If you do not convey joy in your demeanor and gestures and speech, you will not be an authentic witness for Jesus Christ. Delight in what God is doing is essential in our work."

The first question in the Westminster Shorter Catechism is "What is the chief end of man?" What is the final purpose? What is the main thing about us? Where are we going, and what will we do when we get there? The answer is "To glorify God and enjoy him forever."

Glorify. Enjoy. There are other things involved in Christian discipleship. The Songs of Ascents have shown some of them. But it is extremely important to know the one thing that overrides everything else. The main thing is not work for the Lord; it is not suffering in the name of the Lord; it is not witnessing to the Lord; it is not teaching Sunday school for the Lord; it is not being responsible for the sake of the Lord in the community; it is not keeping the Ten Commandments; not loving your neighbor; not observing the golden rule. "The chief end of man is to glorify God and enjoy him forever." Or, in the vocabulary of Psalm 134, "Bless GOD."

"*Charis* always demands the answer *eucharistia* (that is, grace always demands the answer of gratitude). Grace and gratitude belong together like heaven and earth. Grace evokes gratitude like the voice an echo. Gratitude follows grace as thunder follows lightning."[12] God is personal reality to be enjoyed. We are so created and so redeemed that we are capable of enjoying him. All the movements of discipleship arrive at a place where joy is experienced. Every step of assent toward God develops the capacity to enjoy. Not only is there, increasingly, more to be enjoyed, there is steadily the acquired ability to enjoy it.

Best of all, we don't have to wait until we get to the end of the road before we enjoy what is at the end of the road. So, "Come, bless GOD. . . . GOD bless you!"

May it be our blessedness, as years go on, to add one grace to another, and advance upward, step by step, neither neglecting the lower after attaining the higher, nor aiming at the higher before attaining the lower. The first grace is faith, the last is love; first comes zeal, afterwards comes loving kindness; first comes humiliation, then comes peace; first comes diligence, then comes resignation. May we learn to mature all graces in us; fearing and trembling, watching and repenting, because Christ is coming; joyful, thankful, and careless of the future, because he is come.[13]

A LONG OBEDIENCE

An Epilogue

When I wrote *A Long Obedience* twenty years ago, I was a parish pastor writing for my parishioners, the people I knew best in the place I knew best, a few acres of Maryland piedmont on which we were camped for a few years in our wanderings through the North American wilderness. I was doing what pastors do—trying to get this gospel of Jesus Christ into the lives of these men and women with whom I was living, and doing it the only way I knew, through Scripture and prayer, prayer and Scripture. I preached and taught the Scriptures that revealed Jesus. I prayed with and for this mixed bag of saints and sinners that was my congregation, prayed in the name of Jesus.

Two convictions undergirded my pastoral work. The first conviction was that everything in the gospel is livable and that my pastoral task was to get it lived. It was not enough that I announce the gospel, explain it or whip up enthusiasm for it. I wanted it lived—lived in detail, lived on the streets and on the job, lived in the bedrooms and kitchens, lived through cancer and divorce, lived with children and in marriage. Along the way I found that this also meant living it myself, which turned out to be a far more formidable assignment. I realized that this was going to take some time. I settled in for the long haul. That's when the phrase (from Nietzsche) "a long obedience in the same direction" embedded itself in my imagination and eventually became this book.

The second conviction was that my primary pastoral work had to do with Scripture and prayer. I was neither capable nor competent to form Christ in another person, to shape a life of discipleship in man, woman or child. That is supernatural work, and I am not supernatural. Mine was the more modest work of Scripture and prayer—helping people listen to God speak to them from the Scriptures and then joining them in answering God as personally and honestly as we could in lives of prayer. This turned out to be slow work. From time to time, impatient with the slowness, I would try out ways of going about my work that promised quicker results. But after a while it always seemed to be more like meddling in these people's lives than helping them attend to God.

More often than not I found myself getting in the way of what the Holy Spirit had been doing long before I arrived on the scene, so I would go back, feeling a bit chastised, to my proper work: Scripture and prayer; prayer and Scripture. But the *and* is misleading. Scripture and prayer are not two separate entities. My pastoral work was to fuse them into a single act: scriptureprayer, or prayerscripture. It is this fusion of God speaking to us (Scripture) and our speaking to him (prayer) that the Holy Spirit uses to form the life of Christ in us. And it is this fusion that I was trying to get onto the pages of *A Long Obedience*.

Seventeen publishers rejected it. There was no "niche" in the market, I was told; I was advised that it was irrelevant to the concerns of contemporary North Americans. And then InterVarsity accepted it for publication. The risk InterVarsity took gave me a foothold and confidence to continue. And I have continued. Twenty years and twenty-eight books later I continue to write out of this same fusion of Scripture and prayer, wanting to give witness and encouragement to the men and women, both laypersons and pastors, who set out to follow Christ.

A few years after writing *A Long Obedience* I noticed that a lot of people were talking and writing about "spirituality." I thought I knew what they were doing and was delighted that so many allies were showing up in unexpected places. But it turned out that I was wrong. I had read my own convictions into their interests. I thought they were interested in living the life of Christ firsthand; I thought they were interested in Scripture and prayer, the most accessible means provided to us for cultivating that life and maturing in it. By and large they were not. The torrent of "spiritualities" that continues both within and without Christian communities, apparently without letup, has little liking for either "long" or "slow."

Because *A Long Obedience* was my initial venture into what has continued to characterize everything I've written since, this fresh edition seems an apt occasion for making explicit what is everywhere implicit in my books; that men and women who believingly follow Jesus (what we commonly call "the Christian life" or "Christian spirituality") are best guided and energized by a fusion of Scripture and prayer. For as long as an enthusiasm for Christian "spirituality" accelerates without an equivalent commitment to its means, nothing much is going to come of it. There is virtual unanimity among our Christian ancestors that the means consists precisely in this fusion of Scripture and prayer. It is not a terribly difficult way of reading and writing, but it does require diligent attentiveness. The fusion is accomplished by reading these Scriptures slowly, imaginatively, prayerfully and obediently.

This is the way the Bible has been read by most Christians for most of the Christian centuries, but it is not commonly read that way today. The reading style employed more often than not by contemporary Christians is fast, reductive, information-gathering and, above all, practical. We read for what we can get out of it, what we can put to use, what we think we can use—and right now. "We . . . we . . . we . . . we . . ." all the way home.

If we are serious about following Jesus and living out the gift of his life in detail in our bodies and circumstances, we must swim against this whitewater River We and familiarize ourselves with the world in which Jesus and his gift of life are revealed to us. We do it by reading our Scriptures slowly, imaginatively, prayerfully and obediently. Each adverb is important.

Slowly. The Bible provides the revelation of a world that has primarily to do with God. It is a huge world, far larger than what we inhabit on our own. We live in sin-cramped conditions, mostly conscious of ourselves—our feelings and frustrations, our desires and ideas, our achievements and discoveries, our failures and hurts. The Bible is deep and wide with God's love and grace, brimming over with surprises of mercy and mystery, peppered with alarming exposés of sin and bulletins of judgment. This is an immense world, and it takes time to adjust to the majesty—we're not used to anything on this scale. We've grown up on the streets and back alleys of Lilliput—it takes a while for our eyes to adjust. If we move into the Scriptures too fast or move through them too fast, we'll miss most of what is here.

Imaginatively. The Bible includes us, always. Our lives are implicitly involved in everything said and done in this book. In order to realize this we must enter the story imaginatively. We must let our conversations and experiences and thoughts be brought into the story so that we can observe what happens to us in this new context, through this story line, rubbing shoulders with these characters.

We have picked up the bad habit of reducing what we find in the Bible to ideas or slogans or principles or out-of-context "verses." Forget the details; skip the mystery; we want a definition we can grasp and be comfortable with. We depersonalize the Bible into abstractions or "truths" that we can reconfigure and then fit into the plots that we make up for our lives. But the Bible shows us God present and active in and among living, breathing human beings, the same kind and sort of men and women that we are. Imagination is the capacity we have of crossing boundaries of space and time, with all our senses intact, and entering into other God-revealed conversations and actions, finding ourselves at home in Bible country.

Prayerfully. We are taught to read in order to gather information. Our schools train us to read books so that we can pass examinations. We're good at looking for facts. "Knowledge is power," they tell us. Books contain stuff that we can use to get a degree, fix an engine, hold down a job, solve a mystery. But the Bible is not primarily a source of information; it is one of the primary ways that God uses to *speak to us.* "God's Word" we call it, which is to say, God's voice—God speaking to us, inviting, promising, blessing, confronting, commanding, healing. The Bible is not so much God telling us some *thing*—some idea, some fact, some rule—as God speaking life into us. Are we listening? Are we answering? Bible reading is prayed reading.

Obediently. Obediently? We aren't used to this. We have grown up in a culture that urges us to take charge of our own lives. We are introduced to thousands of books which we are trained to *use*—look up information, acquire skills, master knowledge, divert ourselves . . . whatever. But *use?* Well-meaning people have told us that the Bible is useful, and so we pick it up. We adapt, edit, sift, summarize. We then use whatever seems useful and apply it in our circumstances however we see fit. We take charge of the Bible, using it as a toolbox to repair our lives or as a guidebook for getting what we want or as an inspirational tract to enliven a dull day.

But we aren't smart enough to do that; nor can we be trusted to do that. The Author of the book is writing *us* into *his* book, we aren't writing *him* into *ours*. We find ourselves in the book as followers of Jesus. Jesus calls us to follow him and we obey—or we do not. This is an immense world of God's salvation that we are entering; we don't know enough to "apply" anything. Our task is to obey, believingly, trustingly obey. Simply obey.

* * *

I sometimes amuse myself by imagining Friedrich Nietzsche, who announced the death of God and who is now long dead himself, showing up in my study as I'm writing my books. He looks over my bookshelves and sees part of a sentence he wrote as a title on one of the books. He learns that I wrote the book. He beams (although I do have trouble imagining Nietzsche *beaming*). How pleased he is to find that I have kept his wonderful sentence "A long obedience in the same direction" in circulation into the third Christian millennium.

Then he takes the book off the shelf and looks through it. His face furrows into an angry frown. The old atheist was convinced that Christians, by promoting the weak and ineffectual Jesus to keep the weakest, spiritually diseased, morally unfit and inferior parts of the population alive and reproducing, were a malign influence on civilization and would be the ruin of us all. He thought he'd delivered a death blow, and now he finds us still at it.

I love imagining him standing there angry and appalled, beard smoking, astonished that these weak, inadequate, ineffectual and unfit Christians are alive still, and still reproducing.

Notes

Chapter 1: Discipleship

[1] *The Book of Common Prayer* (New York: Church Pension Fund, 1945), p. 276.

[2] Amos T. Wilder writes, "World means more than 'mankind fallen away from God.' . . . The world is created and loved by God, and Christ has come to save it. But it is ephemeral, subject to decay and death; moreover, it has fallen under the control of the evil one, and therefore into darkness." In *The Interpreter's Bible*, ed. George Arthur Buttrick (Nashville: Abingdon, 1952), 12:238.

[3] Gore Vidal, *Matters of Fact and Fiction* (New York: Random House, 1977), p. 86.

[4] Friedrich Nietzsche, *Beyond Good and Evil*, trans. Helen Zimmern (London: 1907), sec. 188.

[5] There is no independent documentation that the Psalms of Ascents were used thus, and therefore no consensus among scholars that they were associated with the pilgrimage journeys to Jerusalem. The connection is conjectural but not at all fanciful. Commentators both Jewish and Christian have interpreted these psalms in this framework.

[6] Paul Tournier, *A Place for You* (New York: Harper & Row, 1968), p. 163.

[7] Thomas Szasz, *Schizophrenia, the Sacred Symbol of Psychiatry* (Garden City, N.J.: Doubleday, 1978), p. 72.

[8] Paul Goodman, *Little Prayers and Finite Experience* (New York: Harper & Row, 1972), p. 16.

[9] William Faulkner, quoted in Sam di Bonaventura's program notes to Elie Siegmeister's Symphony no. 5, Baltimore Symphony Concert, May 5, 1977.

Chapter 2: Repentance

[1] John Baillie, *Invitation to Pilgrimage* (New York: Charles Scribner's Sons, 1942), p. 8.

[2] Elie Wiesel, *Souls on Fire* (New York: Vintage, 1973), p. 154.

[3]Abraham Heschel, *The Prophets* (New York: Harper & Row, 1962), pp. 71-72.
[4]Ibid., p. 190.

Chapter 3: Providence

[1]John Calvin, *Commentary on the Psalms* (Grand Rapids, Mich.: Eerdmans, 1949), 5:63.
[2]Johannes Pedersen describes the situation thus: "The sun and the moon, which meant so much for the maintenance of order in life, often became independent gods among the neighboring peoples or became part of the nature of other gods. Job expressly denies having kissed his hand to these mighty beings ('. . . if I have looked at the sun when it shone, or the moon moving in splendor, and my heart has been secretly enticed, and my mouth has kissed my hand; this also would be an iniquity to be punished by the judgment, for I should have been false to God above'). And in a judgment prophecy it is said that Yahweh will visit all the host of heaven on high, and the kings on earth, and the sun and the moon shall be put to shame, when Yahweh shall reign in Zion ('Then the moon shall be confounded and the sun ashamed; for the Lord of hosts will reign on Mount Zion and in Jerusalem.' Isaiah 24:33)." *Israel: Its Life and Culture* (London: Oxford University Press, 1926), p. 635.
[3]There are, of course, numerous instances when hills and mountains are used as a metaphor for the strength and majesty of God—for instance, Psalms 3:4, 24:3, 43:3, 48:1.

Chapter 4: Worship

[1]Paul Scherer, *The Word God Sent* (New York: Harper & Row, 1965), p. 166.
[2]Herbert Hendin, *The Age of Sensation* (New York: W. W. Norton, 1975), p. 325.
[3]Charles Spurgeon, quoted in Helmut Thielicke, *Encounter with Spurgeon* (Philadelphia: Fortress, 1963), p. 11.

Chapter 5: Service

[1]Walther Zimmerli, "χάρις," in *Theological Dictionary of the New Testament,* ed. Gerhard Kittel and Gerhard Friedrich (Grand Rapids, Mich.: Eerdmans, 1974), 9:377.

Chapter 6: Help

[1]Robert Browning, "Easter Day," in *The Poems and Plays of Robert Browning* (New York: Random House, 1934), p. 503.

Chapter 7: Security

[1]George Adam Smith, *Historical Geography of the Holy Land* (London: Collins, 1966), p. 178.

[2]Gilbert Highet, *Man's Unconquerable Mind* (New York: Columbia University Press, 1954), p. 24.

[3]Alexander Maclaren, *The Psalms* (New York: A. C. Armstrong, 1908), 2:316.

[4]Mitchell Dahood translates: "But those tottering for their devious ways . . ." By repointing the Hebrew consonants he finds the psalmist using the same word as in verse 1 (*mwt*) and so contrasting the one who trusts in God and is a rock-solid mountain that can't be moved with the one who refused to trust in God and therefore slips and "totters"—backslides. *Psalms III* (Garden City, N.J.: Doubleday, 1970), p. 214.

[5]Charles Spurgeon, *The Treasury of David* (Grand Rapids, Mich.: Zondervan, 1950), 6:59.

Chapter 8: Joy

[1]Ellen Glasgow, *The Woman Within* (New York: Harcourt Brace, 1954), p. 15.

[2]Phyllis McGinley, *Saint-Watching* (New York: Viking, 1969), pp. 13-14.

[3]Elie Wiesel, *Souls on Fire* (New York: Vintage, 1973), p. 100.

Chapter 9: Work

[1]Hilary of Poitiers, quoted in G. A. Studdert-Kennedy, *The Word and the Work* (London: Hodder & Stoughton, 1965), p. 33.

Chapter 10: Happiness

[1]Two Hebrew words are translated "blessed" in this psalm. The word used in verses 1-2 (*'ashre*) describes the sense of happiness and wholeness that comes from living in good relationship with God. The word used in verses 4-5 (*barak*) describes what God does as he shares his abundant life with us in a relationship of salvation.

[2]F. Hauck, "μακάριος," in *Theological Dictionary of the New Testament,* ed. Gerhard Kittel and Gerhard Friedrich (Grand Rapids, Mich.: Eerdmans, 1967), 4:369.

[3]Johannes Pedersen, *Israel: Its Life and Culture* (London: Oxford University Press, 1926), pp. 182-99.

[4]Ibid., pp. 193, 211.

[5]John Calvin, *Commentary on the Psalms* (Grand Rapids, Mich.: Eerdmans, 1949), 5:115.

[6]Austin Farrer, *The Brink of Mystery* (London: SPCK, 1976), p. 52.

[7]John Henry Newman, *The Preaching of John Henry Newman*, ed. W. D. White (Philadelphia: Fortress, 1969), p. 77.

Chapter 11: Perseverance
[1]H. Cremer, quoted in Gerhard von Rad, *Theology of the Old Testament* (New York: Harper & Row, 1962), 1:371.

Chapter 12: Hope
[1]Sally Cunneen, "Listening to Illich," *The Christian Century,* September 29, 1976.
[2]P. T. Forsyth, *The Cure of Souls* (Grand Rapids, Mich.: Eerdmans, 1971), p. 128.
[3]Gerhard von Rad, *Theology of the Old Testament* (New York: Harper & Row, 1962), 1:384.
[4]Henri J. M. Nouwen, *The Wounded Healer* (New York: Doubleday, 1972), p. 95.
[5]George MacDonald, *Unspoken Sermons, First Series,* quoted in frontispiece of C. S. Lewis, *The Problem of Pain* (New York: Macmillan, 1953).
[6]Forsyth, *Cure of Souls,* p. 113.
[7]Karl Barth, *Church Dogmatics* 3/1 (Edinburgh: T & T Clark, 1957), p. 369.
[8]George MacDonald, quoted in Denis Donogue, *New York Review of Books,* December 21, 1967.
[9]Augustine, *The City of God* (New York: Doubleday, 1958), p. 46.

Chapter 13: Humility
[1]G. K. Chesterton, *Orthodoxy* (New York: John Lane, 1909), p. 212.
[2]John Calvin, *Commentary on the Psalms* (Grand Rapids, Mich.: Eerdmans, 1949), 5:140.
[3]Artur Weiser, *The Psalms* (Philadelphia: Westminster Press, 1962), p. 777.
[4]Charles Spurgeon, *The Treasury of David* (Grand Rapids, Mich.: Zondervan, 1950), 6:137.
[5]Ibid., p. 136.
[6]Peter Marin in *Saturday Review of Literature,* September 19, 1970, p. 73

Chapter 14: Obedience
[1]Karl Barth, *Church Dogmatics* 4/3, 2nd half (Edinburgh: T & T Clark, 1957), p. 670.

Chapter 15: Community
[1]Philip Slater, in his searching study of the way Americans live together, says

that all of us have a desire and need for community—"the wish to live in trust and fraternal cooperation with one's fellows in a total and visible collective entity. It is easy to produce examples of the many ways in which Americans attempt to minimize, circumvent, or deny the interdependence upon which all human societies are based. We seek a private house, a private means of transportation, a private garden, a private laundry, self-service stores, and do-it-yourself skills of every kind. An enormous technology seems to have set itself the task of making it unnecessary for one human being ever to ask anything of another in the course of going about his daily business. . . . We seek more and more privacy, and feel more alienated and lonely when we get it. . . . Our encounters with others tend increasingly to be competitive as a result of the search for privacy. We less and less often meet our fellow man to share and exchange, and more and more often encounter him as an impediment or a nuisance: making the highway crowded when we are rushing somewhere, cluttering and littering the beach or park or wood, pushing in front of us at the supermarket, taking the last parking place, polluting our air and water, building a highway through our house, blocking our view, and so on. Because we have cut off so much communication with each other we keep bumping into each other, and thus a higher and higher percentage of our interpersonal contacts are abrasive." *Pursuit of Loneliness* (Boston: Beacon, 1970), pp. 7-8.

[2]Martin Buber, *I and Thou* (New York: Charles Scribner's Sons, 1970), p. 62.

[3]*Poems and Prose of Gerard Manley Hopkins* (Baltimore: Penguin, 1953), p. 27.

[4]Dietrich Bonhoeffer, *Life Together* (New York: Harper & Brothers, 1954), p. 25.

[5]Ibid., p. 23.

[6]Margaret Mead, *Culture and Commitment* (Garden City, N.J.: Natural History Press/Doubleday, 1970), p. 17.

[7]Mary Bosenquet, *The Life and Death of Dietrich Bonhoeffer* (New York: Harper & Row, 1968), pp. 15-16.

Chapter 16: Blessing

[1]Charles Colson, *Born Again* (New York: Bantam, 1976), p. 10.

[2]Ibid., p. 7.

[3]J. Y. Campbell, "Blessedness," in *Interpreter's Dictionary of the Bible,* ed. George Arthur Buttrick (Nashville: Abingdon, 1962), 1:445.

[4]Johannes Pedersen, *Israel: Its Life and Culture* (London: Oxford University Press, 1926), p. 202.

[5]W. J. Harrelson, "Blessings and Cursings," in *Interpreter's Dictionary,* 1:446.

[6]B. Duhm, *Das Buch Hiob* (1897), p. 12, quoted in Hermann W. Beyer,

"εὐλεγέω," in *Theological Dictionary of the New Testament,* ed. Gerhard Kittel and Gerhard Friedrich (Grand Rapids, Mich.: Eerdmans, 1964), 2:758.

[7]Ibid., p. 760.

[8]John Calvin, *Commentary on the Psalms* (Grand Rapids, Mich.: Eerdmans, 1949), p. 168.

[9]Eric Routley, *Ascent to the Cross* (London: SCM Press, 1962), p. 72.

[10]Karl Barth, *Church Dogmatics* 2/1 (Edinburgh: T & T Clark, 1957), p. 656.

[11]Charles Dickens, *Great Expectations* (reprint, New York: Heritage, 1939), p. 198.

[12]Karl Barth, *Church Dogmatics* 4/1 (Edinburgh: T & T Clark, 1956), p. 4.

[13]John Henry Newman, *The Preaching of John Henry Newman,* ed. W. D. White (Philadelphia: Fortress, 1969), p. 211.

List of Works by Eugene H. Peterson

In order of original publication.

Growing Up in Christ: A Guide for Families with Adolescents. Atlanta, GA: John Knox Press, 1976.

A Year with the Psalms: 365 Meditations and Prayers. Waco, TX: Word Books, 1979.

Five Smooth Stones for Pastoral Work. Atlanta, GA: John Knox, 1980.

A Long Obedience in the Same Direction: Discipleship in an Instant Society. Downers Grove, IL: InterVarsity Press, 1980.

Traveling Light: Reflections on the Free Life. Downers Grove, IL: InterVarsity Press, 1982.

Run with the Horses: The Quest for Life at Its Best. Downers Grove, IL: InterVarsity Press, 1983.

Earth and Altar: The Community of Prayer in a Self-Bound Society. New York: Paulist / Downers Grove, IL: InterVarsity Press, 1985.

Forces Concealed in Quiet: Meditations from the Writings of John the Apostle. Nashville: T. Nelson, 1985.

Growing Up with Your Teenager. Old Tappan, NJ: F. H. Revell, 1987.

Psalms: Prayers of the Heart. LifeGuide Bible Studies. Downers Grove, IL: InterVarsity Press, 1987.

Weddings, Funerals, and Special Events. With Calvin Miller et al. Carol Stream, IL: Christianity Today / Waco, TX: Word, 1987.

Working the Angles: The Shape of Pastoral Integrity. Grand Rapids, MI: Eerdmans, 1987.

Reversed Thunder: The Revelation of John and the Praying Imagination. San Francisco: Harper & Row, 1988.

Answering God: The Psalms as Tools for Prayer. San Francisco: Harper & Row, 1989.

The Contemplative Pastor: Returning to the Art of Spiritual Direction. Carol Stream, IL: Christianity Today / Waco, TX: Word, 1989.

Stories for the Christian Year, editor. New York: Macmillan, 1992.

Under the Unpredictable Plant: An Exploration in Vocational Holiness. Grand Rapids, MI: Eerdmans, 1992.

The Message: The New Testament in Contemporary English. Colorado Springs, CO: NavPress, 1993.

Praying with Jesus: A Year of Daily Prayers and Reflections on the Words and Actions of Jesus. San Francisco: HarperSanFrancisco, 1993.

Praying with the Psalms: A Year of Daily Prayers and Reflections on the Words of David. San Francisco: HarperSanFrancisco, 1993.

Where Your Treasure Is: Psalms That Summon You from Self to Community. Grand Rapids, MI: Eerdmans, 1993.

Like Dew Your Youth: Growing Up with Your Teenager. Grand Rapids, MI: Eerdmans, 1994.

Praying with Moses: A Year of Daily Prayers and Reflections on the Words and Actions of Moses. San Francisco: HarperSanFrancisco, 1994.

Praying with the Early Christians: A Year of Daily Prayers and Reflections on the Words of the Early Christians. San Francisco: HarperSanFrancisco, 1994.

Praying with Paul: A Year of Daily Prayers and Reflections on the Words of Paul. San Francisco: HarperSanFrancisco, 1995.

Praying with the Prophets: A Year of Daily Prayers and Reflections on the Words and Actions of the Prophets. San Francisco: HarperSanFrancisco, 1995.

Living the Message: Daily Reflections with Eugene H. Peterson. Edited by Janice Stubbs Peterson. San Francisco: HarperSanFrancisco, 1996.

Take and Read: Spiritual Reading, an Annotated List. Grand Rapids, MI: Eerdmans, 1996.

Leap Over a Wall: Earthy Spirituality for Everyday Christians. New York: HarperCollins, 1997.

Subversive Spirituality. Edited by Jim Lyster, John Sharon, and Peter Santucci. Grand Rapids, MI: Eerdmans, 1997.

Not a Day Goes by Without His Unfolding Grace. Colorado Springs, CO: NavPress, 1998.

The Wisdom of Each Other: A Conversation Between Spiritual Friends. Grand Rapids, MI: Zondervan, 1998.

First and Second Samuel. Westminster Bible Companion. Louisville, KY: Westminster John Knox, 1999.

The Psalms: An Artist's Impression. Paintings by Anneke Kaai. Downers Grove, IL: InterVarsity Press, 1999.

The Unnecessary Pastor: Rediscovering the Call. With Marva J. Dawn. Edited by Peter Santucci. Grand Rapids, MI: Eerdmans, 2000.

Allegories of Heaven: An Artist Explores the Greatest Story Ever Told. Illustrated by Dinah Roe Kendall. Downers Grove, IL: InterVarsity Press, 2002.

Epiphanies: Stories for the Christian Year. Coedited with Emilie Griffin. Grand Rapids, MI: Baker Books, 2003.

The Message: The Bible in Contemporary Language. Colorado Springs, CO: NavPress, 2003.

In a Word. With Anneke Kaai. Brewster, MA: Paraclete, 2003.

The Christmas Troll. Illustrated by Will Terry. Colorado Springs, CO: NavPress, 2004.

God's Message for Each Day: Wisdom from the Word of God. Nashville: J. Countryman, 2004.

Christ Plays in Ten Thousand Places: A Conversation in Spiritual Theology. Grand Rapids, MI: Eerdmans, 2005.

Eat This Book: A Conversation in the Art of Spiritual Reading. Grand Rapids, MI: Eerdmans, 2006.

Living the Resurrection: The Risen Christ in Everyday Life. Colorado Springs, CO: NavPress, 2006.

A Year with Jesus: Daily Readings and Meditations. San Francisco: HarperSanFrancisco, 2006.

Conversations: The Message with Its Translator. Colorado Springs, CO: NavPress, 2007.

The Jesus Way: A Conversation on the Ways That Jesus Is the Way. Grand Rapids, MI: Eerdmans, 2007.

The Invitation: A Simple Guide to the Bible. Colorado Springs, CO: NavPress, 2008.

Tell It Slant: A Conversation on the Language of Jesus in His Stories and Prayers. Grand Rapids, MI: Eerdmans, 2008.

Practice Resurrection: A Conversation on Growing Up in Christ. Grand Rapids, MI: Eerdmans, 2010.

The Pastor: A Memoir. New York: HarperOne, 2011.

Holy Luck: Poems. Grand Rapids, MI: Eerdmans, 2013.

As Kingfishers Catch Fire: A Conversation on the Ways of God Formed by the Words of God. Colorado Springs, CO: WaterBrook, 2017.

A Month of Sundays: Thirty-One Days of Wrestling with Matthew, Mark, Luke, and John. Colorado Springs, CO: WaterBrook, 2019.

This Hallelujah Banquet: How the End of What We Were Reveals Who We Can Be. Colorado Springs, CO: WaterBrook, 2021.

BECOMING OUR TRUE SELVES

The nautilus is one of the sea's oldest creatures. Beginning with a tight center, its remarkable growth pattern can be seen in the ever-enlarging chambers that spiral outward. The nautilus in the IVP Formatio logo symbolizes deep inward work of spiritual formation that begins rooted in our souls and then opens to the world as we experience spiritual transformation. The shell takes on a stunning pearlized appearance as it ages and forms in much the same way as the souls of those who devote themselves to spiritual practice. Formatio books draw on the ancient wisdom of the saints and the early church as well as the rich resources of Scripture, applying tradition to the needs of contemporary life and practice.

Within each of us is a longing to be in God's presence. Formatio books call us into our deepest desires and help us to become our true selves in the light of God's grace.

VISIT
ivpress.com/formatio
*to see all of the books in the
line and to sign up for the
IVP Formatio newsletter.*

THE IVP SIGNATURE COLLECTION

Since 1947 InterVarsity Press has been publishing thoughtful Christian books that serve the university, the church, and the world. In celebration of our seventy-fifth anniversary, IVP is releasing special editions of select iconic and bestselling books from throughout our history.

RELEASED IN 2019

Basic Christianity (1958)
JOHN STOTT

How to Give Away Your Faith (1966)
PAUL E. LITTLE

RELEASED IN 2020

The God Who Is There (1968)
FRANCIS A. SCHAEFFER

This Morning with God (1968)
EDITED BY CAROL ADENEY AND BILL WEIMER

The Fight (1976)
JOHN WHITE

Free at Last? (1983)
CARL F. ELLIS JR.

The Dust of Death (1973)
OS GUINNESS

The Singer (1975)
CALVIN MILLER

RELEASING IN 2021

Knowing God (1973)
J. I. PACKER

Out of the Saltshaker and Into the World
(1979) REBECCA MANLEY PIPPERT

A Long Obedience in the Same Direction
(1980) EUGENE H. PETERSON

More Than Equals (1993)
SPENCER PERKINS AND CHRIS RICE

Between Heaven and Hell (1982)
PETER KREEFT

Good News About Injustice (1999)
GARY A. HAUGEN

The Challenge of Jesus (1999)
N. T. WRIGHT

RELEASING IN 2022

Hearing God (1999)
DALLAS WILLARD

The Heart of Racial Justice (2004)
BRENDA SALTER McNEIL AND
RICK RICHARDSON

Sacred Rhythms (2006)
RUTH HALEY BARTON

Habits of the Mind (2000)
JAMES W. SIRE

True Story (2008)
JAMES CHOUNG

Scribbling in the Sand (2002)
MICHAEL CARD

The Next Worship (2015)
SANDRA MARIA VAN OPSTAL

Delighting in the Trinity (2012)
MICHAEL REEVES

Strong and Weak (2016)
ANDY CROUCH

Liturgy of the Ordinary (2016)
TISH HARRISON WARREN

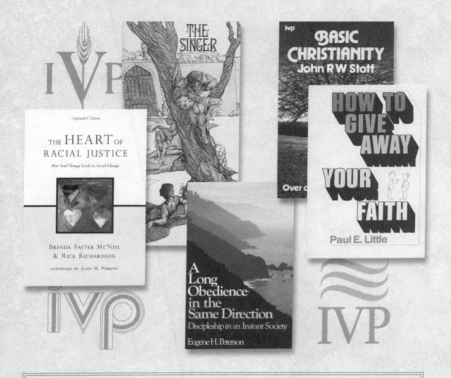

IVP SIGNATURE BIBLE STUDIES

As companions to the IVP Signature Collection, IVP Signature Bible Studies feature the inductive study method, equipping individuals and groups to explore the biblical truths embedded in these books.

Basic Christianity Bible Study
JOHN STOTT

How to Give Away Your Faith Bible Study
PAUL E. LITTLE

The Singer Bible Study, CALVIN MILLER

Knowing God Bible Study, J. I. PACKER

A Long Obedience in the Same Direction Bible Study, EUGENE H. PETERSON

Good News About Injustice Bible Study
GARY A. HAUGEN

Hearing God Bible Study
DALLAS WILLARD

The Heart of Racial Justice Bible Study
BRENDA SALTER McNEIL AND
RICK RICHARDSON

True Story Bible Study, JAMES CHOUNG

The Next Worship Bible Study
SANDRA MARIA VAN OPSTAL

Strong and Weak Bible Study
ANDY CROUCH